PRAISE FOR *A FIELL*

We live in a culture where connection and community seem readily available, yet experientially, we see the rise of heightened individualism, loneliness, isolation, and depression. I couldn't be more grateful for Ben Connelly's *A Field Guide for Genuine Community*. This book will serve as a tour guide for believers as they embark on a deep adventurous journey toward becoming the kind of community, the kind of family, God desires His people to be.

ED STETZER, ***Executive Director, Wheaton College Billy Graham Center***

Are you longing for more authentic, biblical relationships with others? Then you must read *A Field Guide for Genuine Community*. Within a five-week framework, Pastor Ben answers our questions—and our excuses—about developing church connections in your own spiritual family. Through Bible study and pertinent questions, Ben teaches us how to intentionally build intimate and multigenerational discipleship groups that are actually fun to be a part of! Read it, apply it, and see how your church can become less of an organization and more of a growing organism where you can enjoy a deep and fruitful life together.

JANI ORTLUND, ***Renewal Ministries***

If you're done with the façade of community, tired of shallow relationships, and ready to give up on a Sunday-centric faith, this book is for you. I love the way that my friend Ben doesn't just present a couple quick fixes or silver bullets to solve your discipleship woes. Rather, he pastorally introduces the concept of church as spiritual family, which is deeply needed for the Western church.

DANIEL IM, ***Lead Pastor at Beulah Alliance Church; podcaster; author of several books (most recently*** **You Are What You Do: And Six Other Lies about Work, Life, and Love*)***

I'm thankful for this book—it demystifies the purpose of Christian community while doing honor to the complexities of it, and centers the grace of God as the unifying and liberating power we need to know it is real. Full of biblical insight and experiential wisdom, Ben Connelly's *Field Guide* will help you pastorally understand and practically implement stronger and more relational closeness in your ministry context.

JARED C. WILSON, ***Assistant Professor of Pastoral Ministry at Midwestern Seminary; author of*** **Gospel-Driven Ministry**

The social distancing required by 2020's pandemic shone a light on a deeper ideological war taking place across the world. For years we have experienced a mass fracturing of trust and relationships. In these conditions we must rediscover the restorative power of family. When people are starving for meaningful relationships, a loving community is good news. A great resource.

ALAN HIRSCH, ***award-winning author; founder of The 5Q Collective and Forge Missional Training Network***

Jesus gave His apostles clear instructions to go and make disciples. They went and instinctively planted churches—but this was not to abandon Christ's instruction to gather groups of believers as loving families who were all to realize their mutual responsibilities. They were not to be mere passive meeting attenders but to gather in vibrant communities, caring for one another's life and spiritual growth. Ben Connelly has written an incisive, practical, and inspirational book that you will find instructive and motivational as you respond to Christ's command.

TERRY VIRGO, ***founder of Newfrontiers***

Ben Connelly has given us a terrific tool to practically lead people to experience and express true spiritual family. The real-life illustrations and helpful practices found in this guide will help people transition from cultural community to spiritual *koinonia*—from façade to family. In the cultural moment we find ourselves in, this tool is right on time!

JEFF VANDERSTELT, ***Visionary Leader, Soma Family of Churches and Saturate***

You cannot follow Jesus by yourself. It really does take a community around you. Ben's ability to communicate, and to both get to the heart of the issue and address it in practical ways, is more than worth your time. I encourage you to read this book, reflect on it, and apply it to how you're living your faith.

BOB ROBERTS JR., ***founder of GlocalNet and Northwood Church; host of*** **Bold Love** ***podcast***

For years, I've recommended Ben's writings and resources on missional community to church planters. He's lived it and has developed some of the best training to help others figure it out in their own context. As someone who works with church planting organizations but also is helping to lead a network of missional communities, this *Field Guide* is exactly what I need to help everyday Christians experience extraordinary community. It will be the same for you.

DANIEL YANG, ***Director of the Send Institute***

Ben Connelly draws on years of study, practice, and leadership to help church leaders evaluate and reconfigure ministry around distinctly Christian community. Churches are intended to be home in the deepest sense of the word. This book helps us be that.

LEE ECLOV, ***veteran pastor, columnist for PreachingToday.com, and author of*** **Feels Like Home: How Rediscovering the Church as Family Changes Everything**

A FIELD GUIDE FOR GENUINE COMMUNITY

25 DAYS & 101 WAYS TO MOVE FROM FAÇADE TO FAMILY

BEN CONNELLY

MOODY PUBLISHERS
CHICAGO

All emphasis in Scripture has been added.

Names and details of some stories have been changed to protect the privacy of individuals.

Published in association with the literary agency of The Gates Group.

Edited by Mackenzie Conway
Interior Design: Design Corps
Cover Design: Erik M. Peterson
Cover image of friends copyright © 2019 by FG Trade / iStock (1146248069). All rights reserved.
Author photo credit: Tina Howard - Fall Meadow Photography

ISBN: 978-0-8024-2279-8

Originally delivered by fleets of horse-drawn wagons, the affordable paperbacks from D. L. Moody's publishing house resourced the church and served everyday people. Now, after more than 125 years of publishing and ministry, Moody Publishers' mission remains the same—even if our delivery systems have changed a bit. For more information on other books (and resources) created from a biblical perspective, go to www.moodypublishers.com or write to:

Moody Publishers
820 N. LaSalle Boulevard
Chicago, IL 60610

1 3 5 7 9 10 8 6 4 2

Printed in the United States of America

To The City Church—for seeking the depths of biblical community for eleven years and showing me it is possible. Many of the stories in this book are yours.

To Salt+Light Community—this book's concepts fill my prayers for what we will become, together. Here's to the coming days.

CONTENTS

FOREWORD

Christian life together is a wonderful concept and, if walked through intentionally, greatly impacts everyone involved. We need discipleship relationships with multiple people who pour into each other with their strengths and glean from each other in their weaknesses.

Though I played one position on football teams, I had many coaches: a strength coach, a sprint coach, a nutrition coach, and a coach who scouted the opponents. I had an offensive coordinator, a head coach, and my on-the-field running back coach. Each of them helped me become the player I needed to be. Yes, my running back coach was the most valuable in my training, but all of my coaches were needed.

Just as I had many coaches pouring into me during football, many men and women played different roles in helping me become a disciple of Jesus. My mother helped teach me about grace. My cousin Michael taught me about the Holy Spirit. My uncle Miles taught me how to be a family man and transparent. James Mitchell taught me about discipling. Ramon Diaz taught me about being a spiritual father. Roy Anderson taught me about godly marriages. Jeff Reitz and Scott Sparks taught me how to study the Bible. Wayne Atkinson taught me about fasting. Lee Sellers taught me how to serve with your family. I could keep going on, but you get the point.

We all need this kind of spiritual family, living life together, to help us find our true identity. I look at John Mark in the Bible: he was always growing from his time spent with Paul to his time with Barnabas and while serving as a scribe for Peter. He did life-on-life with each of these men, and with the other Christians in their lives. I see the same in the life of Paul: from his first start with Ananias, to being welcomed by Barnabas, to conversations with James, all of these relationships shaped him. I see the same with Timothy: he was trained to be a righteous man by his mother, Eunice, became a true son to Paul, and did the Lord's work with Silas and Titus. All the people in Timothy's life, like Paul's and John Mark's and others, discipled him in close relationships and went deep into his life.

A Field Guide for Genuine Community captures this same heart for followers of Jesus today. Ben Connelly will help you go deeper than just being a church attender, and help Christians form deep relationships with God and each other. You will discover how to pour what the Lord has given you into others, and how to let others pour into you as well. A lot of my own thoughts about life-on-life discipleship and deeper relationships have come from the many talks Ben and I have had over the years. For half a decade, I've watched him help hundreds of church leaders and Christians become spiritual families together. I've seen what happens when people add healthy boundaries, accountability, and deep relationships with Jesus-following brothers and sisters to their spiritual life. I highly recommend you go through this book and let the Lord take you to the next season of growth.

This is an unending journey. If you are already pouring into a person, set the stage for others to also pour into that person while at the same time encouraging that person to pour back into you. This is the true family growth process. Everyone is learning and everyone is pouring. You will all become more like Christ in gaining each other's strengths and learning in each other's weaknesses. If you are currently being poured into, celebrate the strengths of your teachers, and also recognize that you are strong in areas that others are weak—the family needs you as much as you need them! As we all learn together, we all have a greater shot at being more like Jesus in every area.

Go all in. Relentlessly and prayerfully pursue genuine community, and you'll find something great: you'll find your life with Jesus. The time is now! Finish the Game!

Shaun Alexander
2005 NFL MVP, author, disciple of Jesus

START HERE

"Y'ALL"

"WE'VE FILED FOR DIVORCE."

That bombshell froze the room: hands stopped in a bowl of cashews; cups seemed glued to lips. Twelve wide eyes were fixed on Todd and Margo, who had just uttered those words. For a moment, everyone sat in stunned, staring silence. All at once, everything unfroze: unintelligible noise filled the room as everyone started asking disbelieving questions. Cashews were ignored and cups discarded as Todd and Margo's friends hugged them, cried, and slowly shook their heads. For the next hour, the couple explained their decision to their friends and every variety of emotional response gushed out.

Todd and Margo were two of eight people who were dubbed a "community group" by their church's leaders. They had signed up to "connect" three years earlier and had been placed together by a church administrator based on proximity and life stage. They had participated in a "Group Launch" weekend at a lakeside cabin. They had decided that Ryan would be their leader, and that they would meet at Mark and Marci's house. The group had gone through three months of getting to know each other, then had faithfully met in Mark and Marci's loft nearly every week since. They had talked about the pastor's sermon from each previous Sunday. They had asked if anyone had needs or requests; they had prayed together. They liked each other. They laughed together, and sometimes—like they would that night—they cried together. Over the years, they had celebrated each other's birthdays and the birthdays of each other's kids. They had watched Super Bowls together.

In other words, this group had checked all the boxes of "community." But no one—literally no other person in the community group—knew that for over a year, Todd and Margo had felt discouraged in their marriage, had considered (and rejected) marriage counseling, had felt distant from each other, and had discussed separation. No one from the group had seen to the depths of this couple's hurting life. No one from the group was close enough to see the cracks that, to Margo and Todd, increasingly grew. They had each made comments about the other to coworkers; they had both glanced disdainfully at the other during long and silent date nights; increasingly their words to each other were marked by irritation (at best). Eventually Todd uttered the question about a divorce lawyer, Margo sighed and agreed, and the papers were drawn up and signed, the day before Todd and Margo announced to their community, "We've filed for divorce."

Sadly, but commonly, after "The Announcement," Todd and Margo both disappeared from the community group and church. The years of conversation, prayer, and friendship fizzled in a single evening. Group members called, texted, and went to their house a few times, but after a couple months without response, they gave up. They still prayed for Todd and Margo, but as their community healed from the sudden amputation of a fourth of their group, Ryan finally led out in the sad exasperation others felt, "Each week we asked who needs prayer, and they never told us."

The next week a church leader joined the remaining three couples. They were relieved of any pressure or responsibility for what happened to Todd and Margo. They were led through a long talk about how the group could commit more strongly to each other. They were charged to tell each other if anything serious was going on in their lives and marriages. Somber nods filled the room. The leader prayed for the community, for each marriage and family, and that God would help them know and serve each other better than they had known and served Todd and Margo. It was a cathartic meeting.

The next week, the group started getting back on track: they started discussing sermons again in Mark and Marci's loft. They started to laugh and pray together again, and to meet each other's needs. They celebrated birthdays and watched Super Bowls. They asked how each other were doing—now with a little more urgency in their voices and a little more intensity in their eyes. And Todd and Margo were replaced by a new couple who'd signed up to "connect." Things finally seemed to return to normal.

Then six months later, as the group was sharing prayer requests in the loft, Don put his hand tentatively on Sheryl's knee and said, "We need to tell you guys something. These past two years have been really hard on us and our marriage. We've been through a lot. We've been disagreeing more. We want different things. Now that the kids are in high school, Sheryl and I realize we don't have that much in common. We tried counseling a few times. It helped a little, but it just wasn't enough. So . . ." Don paused, sighed, and glanced at Sheryl, who stared intently at her lap but gave a slight nod. Then Don looked around the circle and concluded, ". . . last Friday, we filed for divorce."

THE CULTURAL PROBLEMS WITH "COMMUNITY"

What happened in this group! To be fair, trying to find a single diagnosis would be too simplistic. There are layers of brokenness in this community's story. But the relationships between these couples had stopped short of the depth to which God calls His people. The very term "community," popular in Western churches today, has come to mean everything and thus nothing. So, every church defines its own form and process of community, and every Christian chooses how much they involve themselves in their church's form and process of community.

I lead training for a North American missions agency, which allows me to work with church leaders and groups across our continent and beyond, helping them grow in gospel-centeredness, everyday mission, and everyday discipleship. Since much of the Christian life happens outside of Sunday services, and since much discipleship and mission happens among smaller groups of Christians, I hear a lot about "small groups" (or home groups, discipleship groups, house churches, missional communities, city groups, or other labels churches come up with). It is not uncommon to hear that half of a church's congregation is involved in some form of midweek community. In fact, a 2015 Pew Research study celebrated the fact that "three-in-ten religiously affiliated adults now say they participate in prayer groups or scripture study groups on a weekly basis . . . up 3 points since 2007."[1] Only 30 percent of American Christians in 2015 were involved in a semblance of "midweek community"! But as we walk alone, so many of us wonder why our personal "quiet time" leaves us dry, why we cannot kick some sin habit, and why no one at church truly knows us. Could it be that we have the missing ingredient, but—out of fear, excuses, or rejection—keep ignoring it?

THE BIBLICAL PROBLEMS WITH "COMMUNITY"

Did you know the Bible never actually uses the term "community"? This may shock you, since it is such a common word in churches. Since *community* isn't used in the Bible and thus is not specifically defined, Christians often fall into two camps: some read the Bible through a Western, individualistic lens, while others read the Bible through the lens of the kind of community they have experienced. While both are easy mistakes, neither lead to the others-focused "brotherhood" (today we might say "siblinghood") and the desperate need for others that Deitrich Bonhoeffer described in his classic *Life Together*:

> God has put this Word into the mouth of men *in order that* it may be communicated to other men. When one person is struck by the Word, he speaks it to others. God has willed that we should seek him and find his living Word in the witness of a brother, in the mouth of a man. Therefore, a Christian *needs* another Christian who speaks God's Word

> to him. He *needs* him again and again when he becomes uncertain and discouraged, for by himself he cannot help himself without belying the truth. He *needs* his brother man as a bearer and proclaimer of the divine word of salvation. He *needs* his brother solely because of Jesus Christ. *The Christ in his own heart is weaker than the Christ in the word of his brother; his own heart is uncertain, his brother's is sure.*[2]

The Problem of an Individualized Bible

Most of the Bible's commands that translate into English as "you" are plural in their original languages: they are written to people together, not to individuals alone. So as a good Texan I'm proud to say that most of the Bible's commands are literally addressed to "y'all!" (Yeehaw.) Contrary to some Christian pop culture, the Bible is not "God's love letter to *you*"; it is not an individualistic "guidebook before leaving earth." Rather, the Bible is the story of a unified, pursuing God (the Trinity—Father, Son, and Spirit) and His unified, multiplying family (called Israel in the Old Testament and the Church in the New Testament and after). It's full of commands and stories, of that three-in-one God shaping that many-as-one family into His image—and often using other family members to accomplish that goal.

Look at just two introductions of Paul's letters: "To *all those* in Rome who are loved by God and called to be *saints*" and "To *the church* of God that is in Corinth, to *those* sanctified in Christ Jesus, called to be *saints together with all those* who in every place call upon the name of our Lord Jesus Christ, *both* their Lord and ours" (Rom. 1:7; 1 Cor. 1:2). Reading the Bible as it was written disallows an individualized interpretation, or an individualistic faith or life! In fact, it is impossible to fulfill many of the Bible's commands outside of deep relationship and shared life with other followers of Jesus. We are designed to be dependent on God and others. We need help reclaiming the depth of that dependence.

The Problem of Experiential Lenses

Alternatively, church leaders and everyday Christians often assume that the life described in the Bible equates to our current experiences of "church community." (To some extent, we likely all do this.) We might read Acts 2:42 for example (which describes the early church as follows: "They devoted themselves to the apostles' teaching and the fellowship, to the breaking of bread and the prayers") and interpret it as, "They devoted themselves to the preacher's sermon and a Wednesday group, to sharing a monthly potluck and praying for each other." Sound familiar? Many churches' annual vision series are even shaped around asking for commitment to a version of those things: Sundays, small groups, sharing resources, and serving each other.

But in its early days, God's church did not equate "fellowship" (*koinónia*, the word used in Acts 2:42, that we assume looks like our communities today) to showing up to a church service or event, whether large or small. Being "devoted . . . to the fellowship" has much stronger connotation. Used nineteen times in the New Testament, toward both God and others, *koinónia* denotes intimate, ongoing participation together and deep communion for mutual benefit. The word refers to "the share which [some]one has in anything"[3]; in other words, it paints a picture of the co-ownership and deep responsibility that members of God's first churches had for each other's spiritual growth, health, and discipleship. The "fellowship" God calls His people to looks more like the "commitment-to-the-death" pact seen in J.R.R. Tolkein's *Fellowship of the Ring* than a Wednesday night coffee conversation I can skip if I have a headache.

THERE MUST BE SOMETHING MORE

Whether we read the Bible individualistically or experientially, today's common view of Christian community is a façade of the true level of relationship God created us for. For many followers of Jesus, our view of community reflects the kinds of flippant, surface relationships we see in the rest of the world. Australian pastor and blogger Darryl Eyb ruminated on this with me: "In a world where community is fashioned around sports teams, school associations and hobbies, we are left with incidental, surface-level encounters."[4]

Study after study displays a growing age of isolation, where division and loneliness are increasingly rampant. We have redefined "friends" from "people who are in our lives consistently" to "anyone who 'liked' a picture I posted online." In 2020, the COVID pandemic shined an overt light on people's loneliness and a near-universal yearning for any real connection with other people. It is beyond time to go deeper than today's façade of community and to fight for something deeper than our cultures'—and even our churches'—forms and methods of community. God has so much more for us: we are His spiritual family, both in relation to Him and to His daughters and sons (our brothers and sisters).

Throughout over twenty years of helping lead local churches, I have talked with new believers who read the Bible and see God offer a spiritual family to replace the nuclear family that rejected them for their newfound faith . . . but who are let down by the surface-level relationships they actually experience when they find a church. I have also talked to people who do not follow Jesus and who are pushed further from the faith by seeing how Christians interact with each other—both publicly and online, and privately and in apartment complexes. And I have talked to many Christians who read the Bible, see how God's people interact in its pages, and yearn for that type of committed connection. Then they walk into church gatherings, face a stage, sing some songs and maybe respond together to a liturgical reading, and then hear a sermon before going home. Some walk into a class or group, where a leader asks prescribed questions about the sermon they all heard. They pray together and share some small talk before class is dismissed, or one couple needs to get their kids to bed and the communal exodus begins.

Time and time again, I've heard Christians ask, "Isn't there more?" Many people's experience of God's Church does not match its description in the Bible. They long to be deeply known; they yearn to share their gifts and passions to serve others. They want to "speak the truth in love" to help others "grow up in every way into [Christ] who is the head" (Eph. 4:15)—and to have others speak truth in love to them, to help themselves grow. They wonder if that kind of life together is even possible.

This book gives a resounding "YES!" to those questions. Over the next five weeks, we will see what the Bible says about God's people together. I will share examples from my own church and experiences from across the globe, of believers trying to live as a true, spiritual family in Christ. Through daily readings, a little practice, and weekly group discussion, everyday Christians can recover the vital (and accessible) depth of relationship in which God designed His people to live out their lives of dependence and obedience. Truly a "field guide," my hope is to walk with you on a journey that involves risk, vulnerability, and honesty. Over the coming days, together we will deconstruct our individualistic and experiential views and leave the façade of community. As we do, God willing, we will end our trek in a new destination, experiencing the glorious mountain sunrise of something more real and biblical: life together as the spiritual family of God.

WE ARE A SPIRITUAL FAMILY

Just like we can interpret the term "community" through our experiential lenses, I want to recognize from the offset that we can do the same with the word "family," which is a loaded and broken term for many readers. I want to be deeply sensitive in this. I believe that the all-too-common brokenness in families today is a result of spiritual warfare, as Satan consistently destroys the closest relationships people are called to, and thus downplays the spiritual imagery of God and His people that could otherwise be reflected in those actual relationships.

Later in the book, we will return to the fact that "family" is hard. But if we look at the images God uses for His people in the New Testament, we see that He refers to the Church as His body, as a temple or spiritual structure in which God the Spirit dwells, and as a field.[5] But by far the overarching metaphor for the Church is one of family.

Over and over, God uses different terms to describe His people in familial images:

The Church (together) is the Bride of Christ[6]: Jesus died for *a people*, forgave the sins of *a people*, and is King of that *people*. He is the husband of His Church, not the spiritual spouse of individual persons.

Women and men who follow Jesus are daughters and sons together of God[7]: God is our Father, and each of His people have been adopted into His family, as co-heirs of all His glorious promises through Christ.

Women and men are sisters and brothers together in Christ[8]: Jesus is our shared big brother, the firstborn of His followers; every Christian's primary relationship to others is "spiritual siblinghood."

The Church (together) is the household of God[9]: As I taught the elementary kids in our church family recently, a household is different than a house. The church is not a physical building; it is rather what the "house holds": houses most often hold a literal family, and in a spiritual sense, we are a family of God's people.

MAPPING THE JOURNEY

Over twenty-five days, we will see that God designed His people to be a true, spiritual family. But if your final takeaway is that you should rename your "small group" as "spiritual family," I've done a terrible job. (In fact, I'll tell you a secret: I don't love the term you'll see many times in the coming pages, that God's people are a "close spiritual family." But it is the best term to capture our goal, to capture a church's life together.) Rather than outward semantics or the name of a church program, the goal of our journey is more about inward beliefs and a heart posture that overflows into our relationships with other followers of Jesus.

There are lots of layers to unpack, experiences to deconstruct, and questions to answer as we consider the Bible's commands and examples of that level of relationship and how to apply ancient principles to our fast-paced, busy postmodern lives. That's why this book is written in twenty-five "bite-sized" sections. You might consider each day like an *amuse-bouche*, the first, single-bite hors d'oeuvre at high-end restaurants that prepares diners for the meal ahead. Each daily reading is just that: a unique perspective on an angle of deep spiritual relationships for you to ponder and apply to your life before moving on to the following day. Each day starts with Scripture, briefly explores a specific principle related to life together, and ends with a few suggestions to help you take first steps into deeper relationships.

My children are all in elementary school and are learning six questions to ask as they analyze stories they read: "Who, what, when, where, why, and how?" This book's daily readings follow those questions over the course of five weeks:

Week One (Why) dives deeper into the need we introduced today for true and genuine community. We consider the depth of Christian relationship seen in the Bible compared to what we see today, and why we must move from façade to family.

Week Two (Who) looks at the different elements of God's Church. We'll discuss realistic expectations about interactions within God's family, from the historical and global Church to the diverse, unified Christians we each interact with most regularly.

Week Three (What) examines various biblical commands and examples of discipleship together and helps readers apply them to our own lives and groups.

Week Four (When and Where) shows how the moments and places that we already interact in can be used for this kind of relationship, even in our busy lives.

Week Five (How) combines the previous weeks' content into accessible "first steps," while acknowledging that even the best families are messy.

Each week ends with a glimpse of a church in a specific global culture who is living as family and a discussion guide; as you might expect given the topic, this book is best worked through along with a close spiritual family! Whether a church class, a small group, or simply a collection of friends pursuing biblical relationships, the discussion helps you process, disciple one another, and take steps toward treating each other as family. (If you don't have anyone to read the book with, could it be that the first step God wants you to take is to boldly, prayerfully ask one or two people to join you in it?) The afterword addresses the entire local church family, helping church leaders lead God's people toward understanding and implementing this type of relationship across your church family.

FREEDOM ALONG THE WAY

Before we begin our journey, I want to remind you that the good news of Jesus is both the motive and goal. It's through Jesus' death and resurrection that we become members of God's family at all. It's through Jesus' teaching and example that He and His followers showed us the type of relationships we can have, through the power of His Spirit and even across human common divisions throughout history. It's through the perfect relationship among Father, Son, and Spirit that we know how deep God forms relationships that work together to accomplish His work in His world. It's in the depth of Jesus' sacrifice and service to others that we find the extent to which we can give ourselves for others. It's through God's love, forgiveness, and grace that we can love, forgive, and show grace to others—because family hurts sometimes.

There will be principles over the coming weeks that are easy for you; praise God that He has worked His good fruit in you. And there will be hard principles too—that's OK. The Bible teaches us that love is patient, and so is God. In Christ, He has given us everything we need for *all of* life and godliness—and that includes all we need on a twenty-five-day journey of seeing that there's something deeper than our current view of "community." God's strength is made perfect in our weakness; His Spirit helps us when we are convicted, unable, or doubting. And perhaps someone in our close spiritual family is strong in areas we're weak. Through His power and people, God can help us find new levels of dependence, obedience, and relationship—far better than the words of this book can!

At the end of the day, our relationships with each other are actually less about any human-to-human interaction. They are more about our relationship with God and are venues for sacrifice, sanctification, and discipleship. Above all, life in the family of God is a daily act of worship. So let's find a group of folks to go with us, and let's pray for the Spirit's help in difficult steps on this journey. Then let's take our first step together into Week One.

101 WAYS TO MOVE FROM FAÇADE TO FAMILY

Each day offers ways to turn principles into practice. By Day 25 you will have "101 Ways" to pursue familial relationship with God's people. For each, consider . . .

- ➜ . . . How Jesus changes our motives for these actions, which could otherwise be done in our own power and for our glory.
- ➜ . . . What attributes of God, or fruit of the gospel, is displayed (example: "generosity" or "grace").
- ➜ . . . How each suggestion might become a chance to declare the gospel together.
- ➜ . . . Other "ways" you'd add to the list. Post them with the hashtag, #genuinecommunity, and I'll repost.

WEEK ONE

WHY SHOULD I EVEN CARE?

WRITE A BOOK ON RELATIONSHIPS, IN ISOLATION?

I wrote this book while much of the world "sheltered in place" during the COVID-19 pandemic. At first, it seemed ironic to call God's people toward new depths of relationship during a period we were more isolated than we have ever been! But over time, I found it was not ironic at all: in that season of separation, many people—followers of Jesus and not, those connected to "community" and those who had avoided it like the plague—craved human connection.

Often, the need for deep relationship with others can seem optional: we can commit to a small group . . . or not. We can opt for a church's connection process . . . *if* it fits our schedule and conviction. We can interact with neighbors and coworkers . . . when we feel like it. Many who call themselves "Christian" check boxes and feel satisfied: we attend weekly gatherings, serve in some way, give money, shake hands or give hugs, and feel like we sufficiently connect. But all that changes during times of societal upheaval. We saw a clear example of this as a global pandemic played out: the ability to check the normal church boxes evaporate overnight.

What came from this isolation? Even my most introverted friends—whose first isolated days seemed like their best life now—soon experienced a craving for other people. As the world was quarantined and many churches shifted to digital strategies, Christians realized how deep our need is for relationship. Members reached out for shepherding and care during "COVID time," who had not done so in decades of "normal time." My church saw three new groups start online, digitally filled with people who had been group-less. Neighbors who normally gave only an obligatory nod while scurrying into their homes after a long day instead set lawn chairs in driveways (six feet apart, of course), talked, and watched sunsets together.

Week One asks, "Why Should I Even Care?" Why should God's people pursue others? Why move from safe Bible study answers to, say, risk an admission of a deep sin or need? Why pursue something deeper than casual Sunday morning glad-handing? For all the awful aspects of COVID, the season helped answer these questions. Why should we care? Because, as humanity felt overtly during 2020, we *all* need others. This engrained need crosses barriers of time, socioeconomic status, gender, and ethnicity—and even faith: God created all humans for relationship, with Him and with others. This need is even deeper for followers of Jesus: God created you as a daughter or son, connected to His spiritual family. Most biblical commands and examples of discipleship require the involvement of other people!

There are times when our longing for people and connection, for something deeper than what we commonly think of when we think of church or community, becomes more profound. Week One explains why this need runs so deep and invites us into the Scriptures and history to discover the kind of relationship God empowers His people for—and why we should even care.

"COMMUNITY" IS KILLING THE CHURCH

ANSWER
In Christ, God makes us a spiritual family.

READ
Matthew 12:46–50

WHAT COMES TO MIND WHEN YOU HEAR THE TERM "COMMUNITY"?

In many churches, "community" looks like a small group of people with varying levels of friendship, eating, praying, learning, or laughing together in a living room or classroom. This "community" occurs once a week, for a couple hours at a time. As we learned in the introduction, only 30 percent of American Christians said they were involved in even this type of midweek community. But that's not the only image of community that come to people's minds. The problem with the term "community" is that it can bring to mind almost anything!

Simply put, most people—Christian or not—are involved in multiple forms of community. People connect over their shared love for specific sports teams or events. When a Star Wars movie opens, costumed Chewbaccas and Stormtroopers fill theaters across the world, mutually obsessed with the series. Neighbors come together for the benefit their kids' school; fans follow bands on nationwide tours. Book clubs form and dissolve. Bird-watching or train-spotting clubs meet globally.

A recent commercial for a new Facebook group showed a man at a dog park, discouraged by too broad a variety of canines. He receives a "beacon of hope" (said the ad) via Facebook, discovering a community specifically for basset hound owners, which a voice-over declares "more glorious than a million sunsets."[1]

HOW "COMMUNITY" KILLS THE CHURCH

The examples above are examples of "community" according to our culture. If that's true, a church is merely one option for "community" among many. And any group within a church—Sunday class, Bible study, missional community, prayer group, or ministry team—is simply another option for "community" within the larger "community." You get the point. As we bring culture's view of community into God's Church, we risk treating God's people with the same (or sometimes lower) priority as we would a Star Wars premier or a basset hound meet-up. Below are some examples of cultural community that have inched into the church:

- ➜ Affinity-based community: "I choose church community based on a common interest: maybe people I like or live close to, or any number of other shared preferences."
- ➜ Comfort-based community: "I give myself to others only if the 'cost-benefit' ratio stays in my favor. If someone becomes too needy or takes too much time, I opt out, always 'just for a season.'"
- ➜ Convenience-based community: "I can easily leave one community for another. If someone keeps badgering me about a sin issue I confessed, or if there's a 'cooler' group forming, I'm out."
- ➜ Stage-based community: "Many churches change my 'community' every time life changes. If 'community' is formed around being single, I am kicked out and forced to start over with a new community if God blesses me with a marriage. I start over again if God further blesses me with a child. And so forth."

While affinity-, comfort-, convenience-, or stage-based community are fine in our broader society, they fight the primary image God uses to describe the Church: *His family*! Think of your own actual family; you do not like the same things as each of your siblings. But you cannot trade your family for another you think is "cooler." Outside of unhealthy scenarios, you would not walk away from family members in need. And it's literally impossible for a family to be comprised of a single generation! The family of God described in the Bible is diverse in all these ways. Local churches—expressions of that family—should be too.

We'll explore how this can look throughout the book. But today's point is that the common image of church community misses the relationships God calls His children to, as we see it through our cultural lens. In missing God's true design for His people, we are left with an incomplete picture of God's church and stunted in some areas of discipleship. "Community" just doesn't adequately describe the people of God, in today's world.

WHAT COMES TO MIND WHEN YOU HEAR THE TERM "FAMILY"?

Like "community," "family" means different things to different people. Some of us had generally healthy families; "love" and "support" come to mind when we think of family with images of long holiday meals and laughter. Some had blended families through remarriage, adoption, and/or extended family living together; this may have drawn looks from passersby or added unique dynamics. Some had difficult families; you had to try hard every day to "make it work." Most families experience some mix of the descriptions above. Every family is rich, poor, or somewhere between—or all three in different seasons. Each household is small, large, or somewhere between—or vacillated at times as you gained or lost family members.

"Family" can mean a lot of things. But for most people, no matter the specific images that come to mind, family means deeper commitment and relationship than community. This is neither a new concept, nor an inherently Christian one. Actor Michael J. Fox once said, "Family is not an important thing; it's everything." And many are familiar with the twelfth-century German proverb, "Blood runs thicker than water."

BUT ISN'T "FAMILY" MESSY?

Yes.

(I'm chuckling, tempted to leave this one-word answer and move on to wrap up today's reading, because a family's "messiness" is so obvious. But I suppose I'll elaborate.)

Again, think of your own family: *Are* you like each member? *Do* you like each member all of the time? (Don't answer the second question out loud.) Jesus' disciples were a group of various women and men, with various professions and backgrounds. That sounds messy. His companions were young and old, and from various places. Some were fishermen, at least one was potentially a former prostitute, and one a tax collector. They didn't have much in common. Some were sworn enemies: Matthew, a tax collector, and thus a despised representative of the Roman government, was in the same small caravan as "Simon the Zealot." Zealots' sole passion was ridding Israel of Roman rule . . . at any cost. But Jesus called them both into His band of twelve. That sounds *really* messy!

The first-century churches in the Bible included former mortal enemies, now united into the family of God: "There is neither Jew nor Greek, there is neither slave nor free, there is no male and female, for you are all one in Christ Jesus" (Gal. 3:28). The spiritual family of God is made up of sinful, immature, divided, and broken people. Since people are messy, our churches will be messy. But "messy" isn't always "bad." Those extreme differences are what makes our unity in Christ so amazing!

But I do want to pause to acknowledge some readers' very difficult family situations. Everyone's family has some difficulty, tension, and imperfection, but some families are broken to the point that the considering of God as Father, or thinking of fellow Christians as sisters or brothers, makes them shudder. Some readers may have been disowned from actual families *because* of their faith in Jesus. Over my twenty years of church leadership, I have heard of innumerable family wounds. I've walked with families through heartbreaking losses, rejections, sin, and brokenness. My local church family includes several asylum seekers, some of whom fled their homes because their own parents tried to kill them for following Jesus.

I know there's messiness in every family, but I want to write for a moment to those who might yearn to define their family as "messy," because "messy" would be such an improvement compared to the horror and brokenness they faced:

With as much compassion as I can convey through typed words on a page, I want to put my arm around you, tell you that family brokenness is real, valid, and wrong. I want to grieve with you that things are not as they should be, no matter their magnitude. I want to look you in the eye and free you to feel righteous anger and sadness at things God is righteously angry and sad about. *Broken families are not right*. Hard stop. They do *not* fit within God's perfect creation. But from the second page of my Bible on, broken families are real, the result of sin and the whole-life division that started with Adam and Eve. From blame-shifting, to their son's murder of his brother, to all sorts of strife in every generation since, every actual family is "messy," and some leave "messy" in the dust and are downright broken.

PAST AND FUTURE FAMILIES

In that same posture of deep sympathy, I also want to end today's reading by gently lifting your chin and turning with you to the Bible. We see over and over that God makes messy things clean. We see over and over, God restores and/or replaces broken things. Today's reading in Matthew's gospel displays those realities. While Jesus teaches His disciples, someone tells Him that His (biological) mother and brothers want to see Him. We don't know their motive: maybe they wanted to say "hi," but many theologians think they wanted to call Him to His senses. Rather than running to His literal family, Jesus instead offers hope to those with broken and messy families and calls future followers to instead prioritize His spiritual family, the Church: "Here are my mother and my brothers," he declares, not of His biological family but of "his disciples" and "whoever does the will of my Father in heaven" (Matt. 12:46–50).

By His blood, all sin is cleansed; everything messy can be made clean. In His name, every past thing that holds us in bondage is loosed; we can be free. Jesus' followers are a new spiritual family. Anyone whose parent let them down (so, everyone on earth) can be in an intimate relationship with a perfect heavenly Father, who will never let you down. Anyone whose family saw death and division has eternal life and unity. And on goes God's promises for all those in Jesus' spiritual family.

In Matthew's gospel and the rest of the Bible, God calls His people into a new family that will one day be perfect in eternity and into local churches, which are imperfect expressions of that new family today. Yes, God's family is messy; because of sin, every relationship on earth is broken. But rather than being defined by the past pain of our families, God's family—while still imperfect today—is defined by the promised hope of the future. Jesus offers a *better* family now to the rejected and wounded, which will one day be a *perfect* family. And

101 WAYS TO MOVE FROM FAÇADE TO FAMILY

1 Read the Bible together: walk through biblical books or themes, learning from everyone's perspectives.

2 Read books together: address cultural issues, spiritual topics, and questions, through reading and discussion.

3 Commit to grow together: we all have strengths and weaknesses. Spiritual families care for each other's thriving as much as their own!

4 Commit for the long haul: try to walk through thick and thin, in unconditional love together.

keep hope—Jesus can also restore your broken earthly family. No one is beyond the redemptive pursuit of our perfect, loving Father.

Jesus' view of "spiritual family" is a high one and will only be fully realized in His new creation. In light of our glorious future, God doesn't want His people to settle for mere "community" today, based on affinity, comfort, convenience, or life-stage. He designed us for something far richer, deeper, and more beautiful. It is messy now, will be perfect in eternity, and is based on our common bond of His death and resurrection: God calls us to be His family.

DAY 2

MY BODY, BROKEN . . .

ANSWER
In Christ, God designed His people to need each other.

READ
1 Corinthians 12:12–26

HOW DID YOU "JOIN" YOUR CHURCH?

I grew up in a traditional church in small-town Texas and still remember people joining that church. Whether after a year or on their first Sunday, people walked the red-carpet aisle during the final hymn, and chatted with the pastor for a moment. The song faded, the pastor announced the new members, people clapped, and a Polaroid was taken to adorn the foyer wall. The church I attended during grad school had more of a process: people attended a class, agreed to support the church's doctrine and leaders, and signed a form. (They were still announced with a snapshot, though now with a Kodak disposable.)

Two churches, one unified goal: they got new members. Similar announcements, cheers, and camera clicks. Then church members could do whatever they wanted, as long as they came on Sundays and gave to the offering. (As one pastor I know joked, between those two options even Sundays were less important!) In the Bible, however, the picture of "membership" is not about accountability or liability; it isn't about a finish line or signed form. The word "members" in the New Testament speaks to relationships: it was a starting line for the long race of devotion and discipleship God's people committed themselves to (2 Tim. 4:7).

"MEMBERS, ONE OF ANOTHER"

Rather than joining an organization—like a "member" of a social club or coffee subscription service—God calls followers of Jesus "members" *of each other*! Those in a local church are as integrated into each other's lives—and as vital to each other's spirituality and sustenance—as a right hand to a left, or an eye to a foot. God's church is "the body of Christ." Our mouths, noses, and ears serve different roles in our heads, but exist mere centimeters from each other and need each other. A body's functions are incomplete with any part missing.

With that foundation, reread the apostle Paul's words from today's reading: "Just as the body is one and has many *members*, and all the *members* of the body, though many, are one body, so it is with Christ" (1 Cor. 12:12). A new "member" committing to a local church is like an arm—strong, good at lifting things—offering to serve a physical body who is a missing an arm. To function well, the arm needs a hand to grip its load, eyes to see where to take the object it lifted, etc. That "member" imagery describes the depth of need Jesus' followers have for each other: no foot can declare independence and thrive if isolated from the rest of the body; nor can an eye reject the body parts it sees as unneeded. If we think in terms of literal bodies, such thoughts would be ridiculous!

The physical body makes a spiritual point: God's people need each other. Whether a church has a formal "membership process" or not, each follower of Jesus is a "member," designed to fit a "body." We need each other's gifts, experiences, and faith, and others need ours. In tomorrow's verses, Paul describes this more specifically: "We, though many, are one body in Christ, and individually *members one of another*" (Rom. 12:5). The commitment between God's people is not about legality, finance, or event attendance; it's about intertwined lives and devotion to each other.

THE ONLY IMAGE THAT MAKES SENSE

Only when Jesus' followers realize that our spiritual interconnectedness echoes our very bones, muscles, and organs working together do many biblical images come alive. We cannot "let love be genuine, [or] love one another with brotherly affection" without interpersonal relationship. We're unable to "contribute to the needs of the saints" without knowing those needs and can't often "show hospitality" from far away. How can we "rejoice with those who rejoice, [or] weep with those who weep," without being close enough—physically or relationally—to empathize with that deep joy or pain? These are all commands God gives His people, after calling us to be "members one of another" (Rom. 12:5, 9–15).

The Bible often describes gifts God gives His daughters and sons (Rom. 12; Eph. 4; 1 Cor. 12). Their purpose? "Building up the body of Christ" (Eph. 4:12). We grow in Christ by "speaking the truth in love" *so that* "the whole body, joined and held together by every joint with which it is equipped, when each part is working properly, makes the body grow so that it builds itself up in love" (Eph. 4:15–16). As we'll see later, over one hundred "one another" commands exist in the Bible. Christians can only fulfill them in committed, trusting relationships together. A deep devotion to each other—as intertwined as members of a literal body—is the only image in which those passages make sense. It's impossible to live the life of discipleship the Bible describes in isolation; it's equally impossible if our engagement with "Christian community" is only several dozen (or thousand) people facing a stage, singing and receiving teaching once a week, or exclusively discussing impersonal Bible or theology questions.

CAN THIS ACTUALLY HAPPEN?

When planting The City Church in 2009, we cast a vision for living as a family more than an organization. We would pursue discipleship and mission in neighborhoods and on couches, more than church buildings and from pulpits. Our goal wasn't to be "different" from other churches, but looking like churches described in the Bible.

In The City Church's first decade, terms like "missional church" and "missional community" became more common in Christian circles. But in Fort Worth, Texas, these were new concepts in 2009. I was told this kind of church couldn't happen, that I was idealistic to think

Christians—or any human—would commit to others so deeply. I would counter that we see this in New Testament churches—which, for all their messiness, were closest to the source and thus the purest examples of God's intention—and often heard something like, "That was then; this is now," "Times have changed," "Life is more complex today," or "People are busy."

Times *have* changed. But our individualistic, fast-paced culture is even more a reason to reinforce God's call to "one another." Everyone *is* busy, but only with things we deem important. We believed this kind of church could exist in the US, in the 2000's. We pressed on, a group of twenty people in a friend's living room discussing how this could work. Then I visited Soma Communities in Tacoma, WA, a church that was pursuing a similar vision. (*Soma* is Greek for "body," and the Tacoma church valued the church body living as the body of Christ. The City Church has since joined the Soma Family of Churches.) Through a week of learning from leaders, serving alongside the church family, and living everyday life with them—including staying in one family's home—I saw a living example of many ways the Bible describes churches in first-century Israel, Asia, and Europe, contextualized to the 21st-century Pacific Northwest. The training, examples, and interactions at Soma School were helpful, but I remember the moment in Tacoma I knew Christians could still live in this kind of relationship.[2]

I was up late with my host family, the Uhlers, when we heard a knock on the door. Justin Uhler opened the door, and a baby was thrust across the threshold into his arms. The parent didn't attempt to enter; there was no greeting. From my seat, it looked like a pair of disembodied arms simply pushed a baby into the Uhler house, exclaiming, "Take her. Our other kid fell and we're going to the E.R." The disembodied arms disappeared, leaving Justin holding their baby muttering a stunned "Of course."

There were a lot of surprising things about those five seconds. But what is most seared in my mind is that there wasn't a question from either party. There was no "I'm so sorry . . . I know it's late . . ."

from the parent; there wasn't a moment's hesitation in Justin's acceptance of the living human and unexpected new responsibility. Deep relationship existed. This was how healthy families interact: "I need something, I come to you"; "You need something, the answer is yes. No questions asked." What I saw was love, hospitality, meeting needs, and the entrance of one family into the pain and need of another. The "love" felt (per Romans 12) "genuine."

For ten years, the folks who'd met in a Fort Worth living room pursued similar things. As twenty grew to sixty, we were commissioned as a church. We've since seen a few hundred disciples—some new, some who had yearned for this life—join us. Our church has planted other churches to see this happen in other cities. As I write this, our family and another elder couple are being sent out to start another new spiritual family, and I serve an organization to foster this everyday discipleship across the world. "Church as family" takes different forms in different moments. It's not easy. It means sacrifice and commitment. And not everyone in my church "gets it." But those who do wouldn't trade it for the world; several have said, "We can never go back" to what they experienced previously. I can say with certainty, "Yes, this kind of Christian life is possible, even in our individualistic, post-Christendom Western world."

BROKEN BODIES MADE WHOLE

In early 2012, a piece of my vertebrae broke off into a spinal disc. Pain consistently shot down my left leg as we tried a year of tactics to avoid surgery. We could not, so I spent Christmas recovering in bed while my family feasted, celebrated, and laughed in the next room. (Or maybe they laughed *at me*; it's pretty foggy and I'm sure my painkillers gave them plenty of fodder.) While I recovered, my torso adjusted subconsciously to protect the wound while I slept. The skin, muscles, and tissue healed around the incision, though the actual injury was to a disc. Many who have had surgeries can relate. The interconnectedness, sacrifice, and care of various parts of my literal body are metaphors for Jesus' spiritual body we see in the Bible.

What we believe drives what we do. From the Old Testament's literal tribes beginning from one man named Israel, to the New Testament theme of adoption in Christ, to the imagery of household, family, and body used to describe the church, it's clear throughout the Bible: God's people are more than a community; we are a spiritual family. Today we answer the question, "Why should I care?" saying, "We are made for each other." By God's design, our lives are intertwined with the lives of other disciples, especially in our local church—and that's spiritually true, whether we function in that truth or not. We are each members of a body, and we need other members' gifts. The Bible's imagery of "membership" is far deeper than being announced and cheered for and snapping a picture. We are members of one another. That means that—like it or not—we're in this together, and God created us to need each other.

101 WAYS TO MOVE FROM FAÇADE TO FAMILY

5 Consider your week: How much are you alone? With other Christians? With not-yet-believers? If you're mostly alone, pray for a desire to move toward others.

6 Consider friends: Is your social interaction more online or in-person? Consider how to turn digital "friendships" into personal relationships.

7 Consider idols: Where do your time, money, and resources go? What do you think about during free time? Are those things isolating or individualizing?

8 Consider margin: Is every moment packed? Is there space for others to drop by unexpectedly, or time for someone in need? Create unhurried time for relationships.

ANSWER
In Christ, God's church is more than an institution.

READ
Romans 12:2–13

LET THE CHURCH BE THE CHURCH

"LET BARTLET BE BARTLET."

A turning point episode in the fast-moving, early-2000's show, *The West Wing*[3] was entitled "Let Bartlet Be Bartlet," referencing the series' President Jed Bartlet (Martin Sheen). A memo is discovered from within the White House, criticizing Bartlet's weak leadership. Toward the episode's end, Bartlet's Chief of Staff and close friend Leo McGarry (John Spencer) confronts Bartlet, agreeing that the president is neutral to the point of irrelevance on many issues. After a spirited argument, Bartlett finally says quietly, "I don't want to feel this way anymore . . . I don't want to go to sleep like this." McGarry replies earnestly, "You don't have to." Stirring music starts playing, as Bartlet's conviction grows: "I want to speak." McGarry encourages, "Say it out loud. Say it to me."

The conversation continues as both the music and confidence swell, and the episode climaxes with Bartlet ready to lead boldly and "speak now" on important issues. As the president talks, McGarry scribbles on a legal pad. Finally Bartlet asks, "Do you have a strategy for all this?" McGarry replies, "I have the beginnings of one; I'm gonna try [this] for a little while." He throws the legal pad onto Bartlet's desk like a gauntlet, and we see his words: "Let Bartlet Be Bartlet."

MADE FOR MORE

Many Christians feel like their relationships echo Bartlet's emptiness: We're part of an organization called a "church," like Bartlet held a position called "president." But we don't live up to the potential of what the church could be, any more than Bartlet lived up to the potential of his office. We are pressured into a version of "church" based on experiences with, or expectations of, others. (That was also true of President Bartlet, whose stagnation stemmed from trying to fit the mold he thought would lead to reelection.)

In many churches, people know some people's names, greet each other on Sundays, meet in classrooms or homes weekly for an hour or two, discuss the Bible and mention a few general ways it impacts God's people, and pray or deliver a meal when a need arises. Then we contrast that spirituality with passages like today's from Romans 12, where the early church embodies a whole-life love and devotion, and we know something's missing. We are made for more! Why are Christians—many of whom yearn for the deep, familial relationships we see in the Bible—stuck instead on the surface, unable to dive? One answer stems from recent church history.

A SIX-DECADE SHIFT

Most Western Christians' view of "church involvement" is shaped by a trend known as the "church growth movement," whose foundations are traced in part to American seminaries in the 1960's. Soong-Chan Rah's insightful *The Next Evangelicalism* analyzes this trend and draws this conclusion: The church growth movement's "core principles tend to emphasize the Great Commission [found in Matt. 28:18–20] at the expense of the Great Commandment to love the Lord your God and to love your neighbor as yourself. Church growth principles, therefore, prioritized an individualized personal evangelism and salvation over the understanding of the power of the gospels to transform neighborhoods and communities. They also emphasize a modern, social science approach to ministry, focusing on pragmatic planning process that leads to measurable success goals."[4]

In other words, the movement shifted ministry from the corporate "y'all" to the individual "you," from the places we spend most of our lives to church buildings frequented for a few hours a week, and from stories of fruit to statistics-based metrics. The past sixty years have seen this philosophy infiltrate and reshape most American church paradigms and practices. "With the megachurch model becoming the model of evangelical church success, an overwhelming pragmatism began to shape ministry," Rah explains.[5] And while Christians felt this shift during the latter half of the twentieth century, today most accept it as normal: the church growth movement is the overarching reality we have known our whole lives. But while it's an accepted trend, it has led down three paths that can keep churches from living up to God's calling and our potential:

1. Churches Are More Institutionalized

The church growth movement is part of the reason denominations have declined, and the reason many churches across the Western world have a similar look, feel, and ethos. "When visiting different evangelical churches throughout the United States, a certain degree of familiarity begins to emerge . . . you can sniff out an evangelical church even before describing it in great detail. Part of the explanation [for this] is American evangelicalism's tendency to copy and initiate successful ministry efforts."[6] This blurring of lines speaks of institutionalizing God's church. "Executive pastors," so common today, were unheard of before the 1960s, as were multitiered church staff titles like "director" and "coordinator." Popularized by early adaptors to the church growth movement, these structures are built on the entrepreneurial, business, and organizational management strategies that helped shape the movement.[7] Some churches now operate more like businesses and institutions, rather than bodies and families.

2. Churches Are More Professionalized

As churches institutionalized, the movement also led to more professionalized ministry: If growth is the goal, every experience with a church must be excellent. From venue to music; from preaching to engaging kids; to every other aspect of ministry, growth starts by attracting people, and attracting people means doing everything as well as possible. This requires time, quality, and expertise, which in turn requires paid staff who carry out the majority of the ministry. The "all-in" involvement of God's body, the many giftings God gave to His people, and the need for one another for spiritual growth is thus diminished. Some churches advertise popular Christian bands they hire for services, rather than being led by their own members' merely adequate musical gifts. Others rent billboards where pastors invite drivers to special events, promising an excellent experience should they drop by on Sunday. Instead of servant-leaders equipping "the saints for the work of ministry"[8] in everyday life, many churches are led by a few professionals who do the majority of that ministry, which is primarily received by large groups of non-professional Christians in an ever-updated church facility.

3. Churches Prioritize "Input Metrics"

Finally, this trend—which prioritizes "ministry efficiency," "quantitative effectiveness," and (as you'd expect from its name) "church growth"—also leads churches to define success based on consistent growth in areas like attendance, giving, program participation, new members, and baptisms. To be clear, there is nothing wrong with knowing who is involved in one's church family, and we should definitely celebrate someone's entrance into our fellowship and especially into the family of faith. But as my friend Elliot Grudem, whose ministry Leaders Collective focuses on pastors' health, once asked a room of pastors, "Aren't those metrics similar to a bakery celebrating the amount of flour and yeast that was delivered? Instead of measuring input, would churches be wiser to measure output? Instead of celebrating the number of people who enter, should we focus on stories of people growing in faith and life change, discipling one another, sharing the gospel, and fruitful ministry?"[9]

THE WATER WE SWIM IN

You may have heard the opening of a 2005 commencement speech by novelist David Foster Wallace: "There are two young fish swimming along, and they meet an older fish swimming the other way, who nods at them and says, 'Morning, boys, how's the water?' The two young fish swim on for a bit, then eventually one looks at the other and goes, 'What the [expletive] is water?' Wallace's point is clear: "The most obvious, ubiquitous, important realities are often the ones that are the hardest to see and talk about."[10]

The first verse in today's reading, invites Jesus' followers to "*not be conformed to this world* but be transformed by the *renewal of your mind*, that by testing you may *discern what is the will of God*, what is good and acceptable and perfect" (Rom. 12:2). Today's reading invites us to consider who God calls us—His Church—to be. Have our churches been shaped by "this world"? Is "renewal of the mind" and discernment of God's will needed to become all God designed us to be?

To be clear, some good things came from the church growth movement; a three-year self-analysis of Willow Creek—a leading voice in the movement—found that "the church and its ministries seemed to have the most influence at the beginning of a person's spiritual growth process." But that same study "paints the picture of the church being too preoccupied with the early growing years, leaving the spiritual adolescents to find their own way—without preparing them for the journey."[11] By focusing on the masses, individuals were left behind. I must also say that today's reading is less about church size than mindset. American pastor John Mark Comer explains: "I like the definition of *mega* as '(1) Sunday centric, (2) personality driven, and (3) consumer-oriented programming.' You can do church that way with two thousand, two hundred, or twenty."[12] While today's reading is heady, it's simply helping us know the water we swim in. By institutionalizing and professionalizing ministry, and focusing on growth, efficiency, and certain metrics for over half a century, Western Christianity has increasingly shifted away from "church as family" (a concept we'll explore tomorrow).

Yes, most churches are *legally* not-for-profit organizations, but in God's eyes we are *spiritually* far more. We need a Bartlet-McGarry moment to shake off the paralyzing water we've swum in, to free us for the deeper identity, intentional commitment, and familial devotion we see within the pages of our Bibles.

LET THE CHURCH BE THE CHURCH

Romans 12 is for every Christian—as are other passages that paint the church as a devoted family. You *are* a son or daughter of God, and a sibling to other Christians. They need you, and you need them, whether or not we're "professionals." As part of a church, you are *already* part of a family more than an institution. You *have been* empowered by the Spirit to live out the "one another" commands. You *are* gifted uniquely for building up the body. Bartlet was dubbed "president" at his inauguration. Generally at your salvation and specifically when you commit to a local church, you are

101 WAYS TO MOVE FROM FAÇADE TO FAMILY

9 Forgo your solitary weekend away and invite someone over who's struggling—the company and time will mean the world to them.

10 Find a walking, jogging, or cycling partner: consistently go together.

11 Become the home where others' kids land after school—provide great snacks, a play area, games, and conversations.

12 Become the home where adults want to land too—provide grown-up versions of the prior suggestion!

dubbed a "member of God's family." Let's all play our part!

The questions aren't whether we can conform to institutional expectations, desire to attend some program, or want to care for others and develop deep relationships. The question is if we will live out the identity God already gave us, or choose to settle for less. Will the church be the church, as described in the Bible? Will the family of God be the family of God?

(Can you hear the swelling music and feel the pulsing snare as we close today's reading?)

Will we even risk the opinions of the world around us, and of other Christians who settle for less, to pursue illogical but God-given commitments to each other? Let's jump out of our current stream, into a refreshing and better—even if scary—rushing river. Let's live as the family of God. Let's "let the Church be the Church!"

A GOOD FATHER

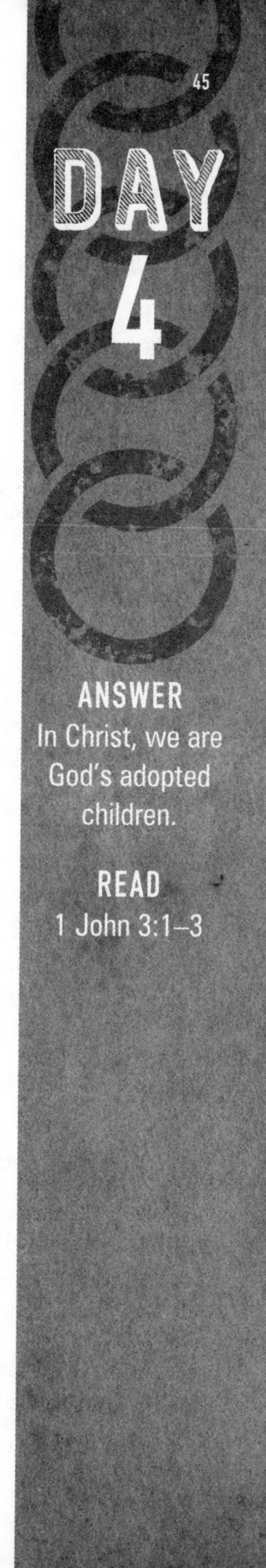

I CRY EVERY TIME . . .

My family is honored to participate in a foster care program called "transitional care." We bring infants and young children into our family, whose parents signed over their rights (or are in process of doing so) and who are awaiting their "forever families" to cross legal "t's" and dot the "i's" for adoption. Every child is different; every story begins in some difficult way. But out of brokenness comes beauty. Every child we've cared for goes back to a parent who has started overcoming the brokenness, or to adoptive parents, many who have waited many years for a child.

The first time we fostered, our own kids were eight, six, and four years old. They fell in love with "Rosie." They each cared for, laughed at, and doted on the newborn. And they were each devastated in their own way when Rosie was placed with adoptive parents. To help our kids understand, we pulled them from school the day Rosie's adoption was finalized. Our agency hosts an annual "Adoption Day," where many children who had been placed each previous year officially become members of new families on one day. It's a party! From bounce houses, face painting, and snacks, to lawyers, judges, and extended family celebrations, Adoption Day is a beautiful picture of orphans being brought into forever families and of joyful parents welcoming kids home.

I tear up with joy every time one of "our" babies goes to a home. Adoption is a beautiful picture of someone lost becoming found; of beauty coming from brokenness. In an ideal world every child would be reconciled to his or her birth parents—but when adoptive parents pursue a child in need, and bring them home as their own, God's pursuit and adoption of His people through Jesus' reconciling work is put on beautiful display.

A VERTICAL FAMILY

This week asked, "Why should God's people care about deep and familial relationships?" So far, our answers are "horizontal," focused on person-to-person relationships. But, while I hope you end this week with a higher view of your spiritual siblings, we must see that the primary reason for living as family is "vertical." It starts with a relationship with God, more than one with other people. We pursue life as a spiritual family because it's who we are, and we pursue it as sacrificial worship to God, our good Father.

A Perfect Father

The concept of God as our perfect, eternal Father is a firm foundation of Christian faith. *The Spirit-Filled Life Bible* notes that "God as Father occurs more than 200 times in the NT and is the exclusive way that Jesus refers to God."[13] God is a good Father, with compassion, lavish love, and gifts for His children. He disciplines, provides for, and honors His children, and answers our prayers.[14] In English, we can miss the fact that in most of the Bible's references to God, He is called *our* Father (plural, not individual).[15] Faith is certainly a personal reality, but only in modern Western culture does it seem individualistic. For most of history, and in most of the Bible's references, He is a perfect Father to *all His children*.

Soma Tacoma summarizes this "Family Identity" of God's people:

> We are God's children (John 1:11–13) who are adopted and fully accepted and loved apart from any good behavior. When I believe the gospel I know I have a perfect Father who loves me and accepts me not because of what I've done but

> because of what Christ has done. This leads me to worship God as Father and obey his word because I love him. I don't obey God in order to be loved by him. I obey God because he loved me while I was still his rebellious enemy.[16]

Spiritual Siblings

With God as our collective Father, it should not surprise us that He defines His children as spiritual siblings. Blueprint Church in Atlanta, Georgia, captures this sentiment beautifully in one of its church-wide DNA marks: "We aim to create a culture of people who are responsible siblings." Their website explains this statement: "We are family. And as family, we actively take responsibility for one another."[17]

I'm writing this while sitting on my in-law's porch at sunrise. I'm sipping coffee my father-in-law brewed. (It's too weak for my taste, a consistent, teasing debate.) My kids are sleeping in beds my in-laws bought, in a house they paid for. Last night we ate food my brother-in-law purchased, while the adults enjoyed drinks my family brought. We took turns checking on the six kids and holding my one-year-old nephew. When my immediate family leaves, we will not be billed for our portion of the food; nor will my kids charge their aunt and uncle for watching their son. Why? Because we're family, not hotel guests, restaurant patrons, or the Baby-sitters Club. Yes, various members of both Jess' and my extended families have different viewpoints on issues from money to politics to child-rearing (even coffee strength). Different upbringings and worldviews lead us to different values and priorities. Conflicts arise occasionally; we deal with some and sweep others under the rug. But despite our differences, we are bonded by something deeper than affinity and convenience. We are here for each other; we pitch in; we live as family.

Your family relates in a certain way, with some ups and some downs. But Blueprint Church's and Soma Tacoma's statements apply some healthier marks of a literal family to the spiritual family of God. Our perfect Father is the source of our "siblinghood." Family is vertical more than horizontal. We pursue a spiritual family, in worship and obedience to God. "We love because he first loved us" (1 John 4:19). "For at one time you were darkness, but now you are light in the Lord. Walk as children of light" (Eph. 5:8). God doesn't just command His children to relate to each other in these ways; by His Spirit, He empowers us to live out those commands: "His divine power has granted to us all things that pertain to life and godliness, through the knowledge of him who called us to his own glory and excellence" (2 Peter 1:3).

Based on their Family Identity statement above (more vertical), Soma Tacoma describes their (horizontal) life of spiritual siblinghood:

> We are God's chosen people—His family—set apart to live in such a way that the world would know what he is like. Through faith in Jesus we believe we are Children of God and brothers and sisters with each other. As God's family we see it as our obligation to personally care for the needs of one another—both physically and spiritually. We disciple, nurture and hold each other accountable to Gospel life together. We do this through regularly gathering together for celebration, consistent involvement in a DNA group, and loving others in the path of our life like the Father loved us . . .
>
> As children of God we love one another as brothers and sisters. Jesus said this is the way the world will know that we are his disciples—by our love for one another. Paul said we were to be imitators of God as dearly loved children who love one another (Eph. 5:1–2). The primary means by which we show the world what God is like and give tangible proof of the Gospel's power to save is through our love for one another. If we don't love one another, we show that we don't know and love God (1 John 4:7–21).[18]

As we pursue the depth of commitment and relationship we've seen this week, horizontal benefits cannot be the ultimate starting point for this pursuit. The primary reason we live as a devoted spiritual family is vertical: our relationships with one another are overflows of worship and obedience to our perfect Father.

WORSHIP MEANS GIVING

My sister lives near me. If my phone rang at 3 a.m., and Caitlin told me her car broke down while she was driving, there is no question in my mind what I would do. I would immediately go help, no questions asked. (Except for why she was driving at 3 a.m. once I knew she was finally safe!) Would it inconvenience me? Yes. Would I rather stay asleep? Absolutely. But no part of me would consider asking her to call back in a few hours, or telling her I'd be there after I slept, showered, and had a nice, leisurely cup of coffee! I am willing to be inconvenienced for the people I love. No one *prefers* inconvenience, but we all have people for whom we're *willing* to face inconvenience.

When thinking of worship, Christians don't often think of inconvenience; even less would we think of sacrifice. "Worship" for most of us means singing a few songs on a Sunday. But—while God's people did sing throughout the Bible—the worship the Bible describes was not songs; they were sacrifices. God's people literally offered God bulls, sheep, goats, and/or birds from their flocks, on a regular—at times daily—basis. They burned grain from their field on an altar. Leviticus 1–7 describes these sacrifices, and every animal or grain-head offered meant the loss of some income or provision. God's people brought gold and jewels—a conservative equivalent of over $32 million today![19]—and gave time and skill, to build God's tabernacle during Israel's desert wanderings (Ex. 35–38).

But in the days of Old Testament prophets, God rebuked His peoples' material sacrifices: "I have had enough of burnt offerings of rams and the fat of well-fed beasts; I do not delight in the blood of bulls, or of lambs, or of goats" (Isa. 1:11). Why would God say this? On one hand these acts had become empty rituals; the vertical had lost its meaning. On the other hand, they had forgotten the horizontal! While Israel still brought offerings, they neglected the relational sacrifice God designed for His people: "Learn to do good; seek justice, correct oppression; bring justice to the fatherless, plead the widow's cause" (Isa. 1:17). God charged them to replace their empty acts of vertical offerings with horizontal acts of love and kindness. This—selflessly giving one's life for others—God told Israel, was worship.

The apostle Paul emphasized the same sentiment for the Church: "Therefore, I urge you, brothers and sisters, in view of God's mercy, to offer your bodies as a living sacrifice, holy and pleasing to God—*this is your true and proper worship*" (Rom. 12:1 NIV).

THE RIGHT SOURCE AND GOAL

The rest of this field guide considers the life God calls His people to, and we will consider how our lives can follow God's commands today. We will consider what devotion to others means and tangible ways to live as spiritual siblings. But today, we simply need to understand that, as great as other people are and as much as selflessness

101 WAYS TO MOVE FROM FAÇADE TO FAMILY

13 Serve the city together: whether schools, neighborhoods, or non-Christian organizations, bless people, display the gospel, and serve with your sisters and brothers.

14 Serve orphans together: care for vulnerable kids, reflecting God's familial heart and bringing others into that endeavor together.

15 Serve widows together: pursue the prior suggestion, but for older populations. Adopt a nursing home or care for the elderly.

16 Serve refugees or asylum seekers together: Agencies can help you meet them; show them the city, teach and care for them, and invite them to meals and holidays.

and meeting needs is beneficial to others, the horizontal plane is neither the start nor the end of the life God calls us to; it's neither the right source nor the right goal.

We are family because we are daughters and sons of God. We commit ourselves to—and sacrifice ourselves for—each other, primarily as worship and obedience to Him. God our Father—through the work of God the Son and the empowerment of God the Spirit—is the only right source and right goal of our selfless devotion to our spiritual siblings.

What does that life look like? We will start to see in next week's readings.

WEEK ONE IN ACTION

The last day of each week you will read how churches across the world live as a family and discuss this week's content with others reading this book with you. As you discuss the questions, be honest with yourself and others, and let them speak truth in love as you put this book into practice together.

LIVING AS FAMILY: SOMA FUCHU, TOKYO, JAPAN

My family has been doing life together with a group of four other families and a few single adults, all of whom had different beliefs from us when we first met. Not one of them had ever held a Bible in their hands or had ever heard of the gospel. This is very common in our exclusive culture where "new" beliefs and religions from the outside are shut out. Despite these differing backgrounds and beliefs, we continued to invite these neighbors into our life. We have fun together; we celebrate and even plan our vacations together. And we open the Bible together to share Jesus.

We also share in each other's struggles. One family had some major difficulties, and they came to us for help. I still remember that we went to their house to talk until late one night. Sometime shortly after that, the wife became a follower of Jesus. She shared with us that she believed in Jesus. She then said, "Yoshi, it is now time for my baptism, right?" She had watched how people in the community came to know Jesus and witnessed their baptisms. She did not need to go through baptism class because she already knew the content. She knows now how to read her Bible and how to do life as a family on mission together. Her baptism ceremony was like her commissioning.

When her husband went away for six months for work, we took care of her and the kids. We just recently heard that this family will soon be moving far away. We were all bawling our eyes out, including the kids. So we decided to spend our last time together camping up in the mountains this last week. I have never felt so sad and yet so joyful at the same time. Our time together these last eight years has been so rich. Now our dear friends who were part of our life are moving away to a small town where there are no Christians.

Many people have come to love this community where they can be heard and experience the richness of helping one another and enjoying life together. Now we are seeing more of these communities that display the kingdom of Jesus starting to form throughout Tokyo!

Yoshito Noguchi

101 WAYS TO MOVE FROM FAÇADE TO FAMILY

17 Share a hobby with people in your close spiritual family; you may actually like books, soccer, mixology, or bird watching!

18 Help your close spiritual family with housework—and when you're doing chores, ask for help. Have good conversation while you work.

19 Borrow tools, ingredients, or whatever else—sometimes the first step into relationship is admitting needs.

20 When someone has a need, small or large, share the burden. You won't often regret doing so.

"WHY" QUESTIONS TO DISCUSS

- [ ] **GENERAL**: What impacted you most this week? What was new, convicting, difficult, or confusing? What biblical truths do you need others to remind you of, in love?

- [ ] **GENERAL**: On a scale of 1–5, where would you rank your pursuit of deep, honest, "familial" relationships with other Christians, and why? (Let's say 1 is "I'm horrible," and 5 is "The Acts 2 church ain't got nothin' on me.")

- [ ] **DAY 1**: How has involvement in cultural or societal groups shaped your view of "community," and how does that impact your view of relationships in the Church?

- [ ] **DAY 1**: How is "family" a better term than "community" for the relational depth God calls His people to? What keeps you from pursuing that depth?

- [ ] **DAY 2**: What gifts has God given you for building up others, and how do you feel those are being fostered and deployed for that purpose?

- [ ] **DAY 2**: What gifts has God given others that bolster you in your weaknesses? How can you celebrate those gifts, admit your need for others, and thank God for them?

- [ ] **DAY 3**: What positive things to celebrate and negative things to lament came from the church growth movement and the ways it shapes our view of church?

- [ ] **DAY 3**: What steps can you take to move from an institutionalized view of church toward a familial view, from a professionalized view of ministry toward everyone's involvement, and from "input" metrics in your church or group toward "output" metrics?

- [ ] **DAY 4**: How is it easy for you to view God as an unconditionally loving Father? How is it difficult, and how can others meet you in those difficulties?

- [ ] **DAY 4:** How is it easy to see other Christians as sisters and brothers as a diverse, unified family? How is it difficult, and how can others meet you in those difficulties?

- [ ] **GENERAL:** What sacrifices and shifts need to occur in your heart to pursue familial relationships with fellow believers—and how can each be an act of worship to God?

- [ ] **GENERAL:** Look over this week's "101 Ways." What else could you do, per your own gifting, spiritual family, and mission field to live as God's family? Post ideas with the hashtag, #genuine community.

WEEK TWO

WHO IS MY SPIRITUAL FAMILY?

I AM THE OLDEST OF THREE CHILDREN.

(Now all you "birth-order" folks can profile me, likely correctly.) My mom was the middle of five; my dad, the second youngest of *eight!* (Good luck profiling that; my dad's youngest brother was in the same grade as his own nephew, the son of his oldest brother! #mindblown) Jess, my wife, is the youngest of three siblings. Her dad was also one of three; her mom, one of five. Jess's and my siblings all have growing families; at the time of writing, my three kids have twelve cousins, with more on the way.

While you likely don't care about the makeup of my immediate and extended family, Week Two answers the question, "Who is my church family?" Similar to each of our own family trees, God grafted His people into one big spiritual family tree. Like any family tree, His has different branches, and on those branches hang different-sized clusters of fruit. From there the metaphor breaks down (as any does). But it's those disciples we are closest to and/or those who we interact with most regularly that we can consider our close spiritual family. As we saw in last week's readings, for their sake and ours we must live our lives devoted to God and to those in our close spiritual families.

In other words, there are different types of relationships and different levels of closeness between followers of Jesus. And of course, there are lots of varied personalities, backgrounds, stories, and even needs and differences we must consider in knowing how God calls us to interact in His family. Examining these realities can help us commit deeply to a few fellow disciples, without adding overwhelming pressure to commit on that deep level to every single Christian we ever come across.

So ask God to open your eyes and heart to His truth, then turn the page as we start to answer from God's Word, "Who is my spiritual family?"

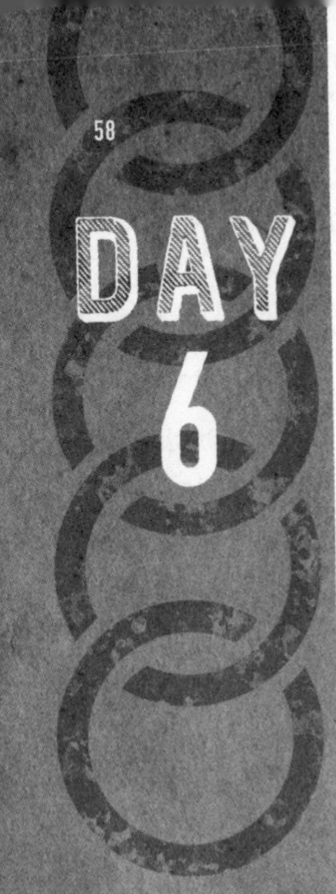

ANSWER
Your spiritual family includes the people you deeply devote yourself to.

READ
Titus 2:1–9

GOD'S FAMILY TREE

HISTORY ENTHRALLS ME . . . SOMETIMES.

In 2016 I joined the masses for a free trial of Ancestry.com. I was initially amazed at the connections that were quickly made, and the generations that appeared before my eyes. It was interesting to discover names, professions, and even newsworthy events from my heritage that I never knew. Before long though, the historical data became spotty. The information decreased, and the names and dates seemed distant and impersonal.

Before the trial (and my patience) ran out, I discovered one side of my family heritage back to the 1700s in Ireland and the other to the 1600s in Germany. But I would never meet most of the names on the screen. The majority are, of course, dead. And the number of great-aunts, second cousins, and so forth combined with the distance and disconnection between us means there is virtually no actual relationship with several branches of my family tree.

The same principle is true when considering our spiritual family tree: in some ways, every follower of Jesus is deeply connected to every other—as we said last week, we are one spiritual family. But it is impossible to live in familial relationship with every member of our spiritual family. Today we relieve that tension by examining God's family tree.

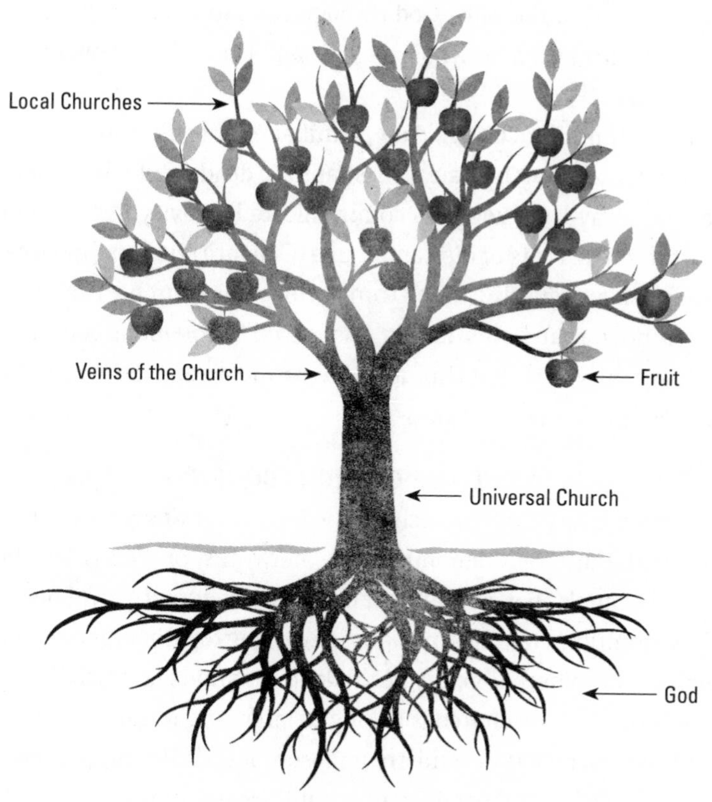

GOD AND THE UNIVERSAL CHURCH (THE ROOTS AND TRUNK)

Ephesians 4 reads, "There is one body and one Spirit—just as you were called to the one hope that belongs to your call—one Lord, one faith, one baptism, one God and Father of all, who is over all and through all and in all" (4:4–6). The overarching theme is that Christians are "one"—we are one big family spanning the globe that will continue until Jesus (our "big brother," Rev. 1:5) returns. We might say that our triune God is the root of this family tree. From that root, "spiritual DNA" runs through all God's people; the global, historical, universal Church is the trunk of God's family tree. We are all made in His image, for His glory. We have the same Scriptures and Spirit. We pursue the same mission, and while it looks different around the world, we worship the same God through the same risen Christ. We are united with everyone who ever has, and ever will, follow Jesus. That's amazing!

But we cannot function in daily, familial relationships with most of the universal Church. Many Christians are dead, while the majority live far away from you, and communicate in ways you could not understand. The roots of our family tree (God) are our "one" source; they nourish and give life to the trunk (universal Church). The trunk is a reminder that God's family has grown throughout centuries and across the world. But through history and across the world, the trunk has sprouted branches.

VEINS OF THE CHURCH (BOUGHS)

Boughs are large tree branches. The boughs of God's family tree might be the different denominations, networks, or "veins" of the universal Church that have grown over time. Alternatively, boughs might be multiple churches in one area, working together for the good of their cities. Whether large, global denominations or small, localized networks, many churches belong to larger organizations united around specific beliefs or ministry philosophies, and/or support each other's ministries, and band together for the common good.

Whether grouped by organization or proximity, these churches are part of God's family tree. Like every family tree, a unified DNA courses through each bough. But each bough grows a little differently: an area's culture or a set of beliefs shape different boughs uniquely. Churches, their leaders, and their members interact more closely with the churches, leaders, and members of their own organization and/or their own city, than with others. We could play out the image to discuss cross-pollination, as some Christians move from one bough to another: a church hires a new staff member, a Christian moves to a new city for a job or a new country for mission. But many organizations and cities include hundreds, if not thousands, of other Christians. At this "bough" level, Christians can support each other—possibly through prayer and funding, and a loose knowledge of each other. But we can't live as family with everyone on our "big branch." We must take a further step.

LOCAL CHURCHES (TWIGS)

Every child knows the difference between boughs and twigs; they can break a twig off a tree, but boughs are too big. The smaller twigs that sprout from a tree's boughs are an image of local churches. Here we see closer, more consistent relationships—where Christians can start operating with deeper commitment. Each local church has specific ways of doing things: its leaders and members share regular interactions, know each others' needs, and have a unique culture and (if you will) specific strands of the larger DNA. Most fruit in a Christian's life grows on the twig of a local church. Because in a local church, Christians start interacting as family.

In various traditions, priests are called "fathers" over a specific local congregation. We saw last week that the local church is "the household of God." And in today's reading, Paul charges members of each local church to treat each other like members of a literal nuclear family. God designed every local church to be comprised of both "older" and "younger men," and "younger" and "older women." These care deeply for each other, serve and teach each other, and work together for mutual discipleship on God's mission. In Paul's letter to Timothy, God's view of local church relationships is more overt: "Do not rebuke an older man but encourage him as you would a father, younger men as brothers, older women as mothers, younger women as sisters, in all purity" (1 Tim. 5:1–2). If I haven't said it enough already, Christians are the family of God!

WHERE FRUIT GROWS

Back to Ancestry.com. I know the "twigs" of my literal family tree best. If you count my parents and Jess's, our siblings and their spouses, our twig currently includes ten adults and fifteen kids. But even those twenty-five souls live in seven different households; and as we might expect, each nuclear family has the closest, most consistent, most committed relationships with one another.

Psychologist Suzanne Degges-White summarizes four common levels of friendship:

- Acquaintances are those we "'sort of know,' at least well enough to make idle small talk."
- Casual friends are "those with whom you spend time within shared activities or with whom you cross paths on a regular basis."
- Close friends are "ones that you call when life sucks so bad that you just want to cry, hide, or run away." They are "those you trust with many of your secrets and the friends who put up with you even when you're in a lousy mood."
- And intimate friends are those "you let into the inner sanctum of your heart and mind, who you trust with the deepest secrets, and who you know will never let you down or betray your trust."[1]

Many Christians' relationships exist at the "acquaintance" or "casual friend" level; church gatherings and programs often promote those kinds of relationships. But that's not the kind of relationship we're pursuing in this book. According to Degges-White's article, "Data from a brand new study . . . of adults from their thirties to their seventies makes it clear that the number of close friends we need to feel that we have enough is somewhere between three and five."[2]

British anthropologist Robin Dunbar similarly explained to *The New Yorker* that people can generally have a social group of about 150 people ("acquaintances," per Degges-White's categories). We can have around fifty casual friends, and around fifteen close friends. Per the *The New Yorker* article, "The most intimate Dunbar number, five, is your close support group. These are your best friends (and often family members)."[3] Even Jesus interacted with different-sized groups, with different levels of intimacy. He preached to the masses—on the mount, from boats and in different towns, and at least once to "about five thousand men, besides women and children" (Matt.

14:21). But Jesus had about seventy-two people committed to following Him. Within those seventy-two, He of course had twelve apostles, with whom He had deeper and more regular discussions than with the seventy-two. But His most intimate conversations and deepest revelations were reserved for Peter, James, and John; Jesus had an "inner circle" of three.

"WHERE FIVE TO FIFTEEN GATHER . . ."

From family trees, to psychology, to Jesus' example, to our own experiences, today's reading simply recognizes that there are different levels of relationship and friendship humans can have. Those deeper, closer friendships—the five to fifteen intimate or close friends; the three to twelve who Jesus walked most closely with—are the deepest, closest, most transformative, and most needed.

The average church in the US in the late 2010s involved eighty to one hundred people.[4] That puts them in the "social" range of Degges-White's categories. The church growth movement (see Day 3) actively prioritizes involving more and more people. This is echoed by the numerous church leaders who strive to "break the 200 [person]

101 WAYS TO MOVE FROM FAÇADE TO FAMILY

21 When going to the park, zoo, or errands, take someone along.

22 When considering a gym or club membership, consider where your close spiritual family are members.

23 When you or your kids sign up for sports or hobbies, join a team or club with your close spiritual family.

24 Join the same social or professional organizations as people in your close spiritual family.

barrier," which the church growth movement calls a common "growth hurdle." Is it telling, per today's reading on size dynamics, that researcher and church leader Ed Stetzer writes, "The most common [church size barriers] are found at 35, 75, 125, and 200"?[5] Perhaps God's priority would not be for His churches to break these barriers and get larger—at least not unless those leaders make sure His people are truly, deeply known and loved, whatever their church's size.

We cannot pursue deep discipleship and life together with dozens or thousands of people! We cannot commit to know, care for, give to, and receive from more than five to fifteen sisters and brothers. Jesus said, "Where two or three are gathered in my name, there am I among them" (Matt. 18:20). This knowledge allows followers of Jesus to be released from the pressure of knowing everyone in their churches; church leaders can equip people for deeper and more intentional relationships that exist at the "close" or "intimate" levels. As we'll see in the rest of the book, Christian discipleship happens best in that kind of relationship; it's how we see true growth in the Bible.

The Christian life is one of devotion, and true devotion can only happen at the "close" and "intimate" level. Perhaps this might drive us toward smaller churches or cause us to more highly prioritize smaller groups within larger churches—combined with church leaders equipping members to "be the church" within those smaller groups. That's where familial commitment can truly occur.

While it's helpful to know we're part of something bigger (the trunk and boughs of God's family tree), and while it's important to remember the global and historic elements of our faith, fruit grows on the twigs. No matter how large a church is, God's people are created for something smaller—deep, intentional, and strong relationships, on God's mission with a few spiritual siblings. That's what most of us can commit to. It's the environment where we can interact regularly. It's how our hearts and minds are wired. And it's where true fruit grows.

NO "I" IN TEAM

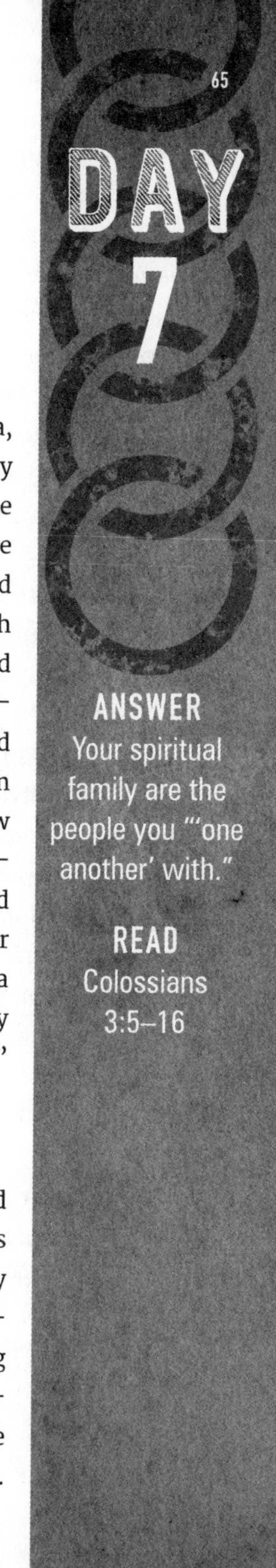

"I CAN DO IT MYSELF."

Travis, my five-year-old, stood by the sofa, clearly forming a plan. He is my most solidly built child but was about to embark on a task he could not complete: lifting the sofa to retrieve his lost toy. I realized what he was doing and asked if he needed help. He looked at me—with far more confidence in himself than ability—and said firmly, "I can do it myself." Then he squatted down, grasped the underside of the sofa, and lifted with all his might. The sofa didn't even think about budging. He lifted again, tried new positions, and grunted under his strain, determined to succeed. I smiled at his effort and waited for what I knew would come. Sure enough, after a minute he turned to me and asked (like it was a new idea; as if I had not offered my services sixty seconds earlier), "Daddy, can you help me?" With an amused chuckle, of course I did.

"I *CAN'T* DO IT MYSELF."

In that moment (and many others Jess and I have with our kids—every parent knows this exchange), Travis reflected a tendency in every human: *I can do it myself*. Especially in our individualized culture, our mindset feels something like this: "For *me* to accomplish what *I* want to—or at least, what *I* think is expected of *me*—*I* have to work hard. *I* have to study to make the grade.

I have to be appropriately involved in activities *I'm* good at. *I* have to 'pull *myself* up by *my* bootstraps,' and *I* have to make *my* own success. Assuming *I* do, *I* gain the lifestyle I want, and *I* can amass resources *I've* earned, to use as *I* wish."

That may be overstated, and *I* intentionally overused "*I's*" in that summary. But we resonate with the sentiment (even if we've never said it aloud) because it's ingrained in our culture, worldview, and minds. High school graduates are ranked on individual academic performance. We are hired, fired, promoted, or demoted per individual work performance. We care for individual houses or apartments, pursue our individual happiness, live individual lives, and so forth. We hear phrases like, "Look out for number one" (meaning, "Take care of your own interests first") and "Do what's best/right for you." In nearly every aspect of life, we apply my five-year-old's logic, "I can do it myself."

The problem? Even outside of our overtly spiritual pursuits, we *cannot* do it ourselves. Those individually ranked high schoolers had a community of teachers, administrators, peers, and, often, family support that shaped their multiyear education. In any organization with multiple employees, the roles, relationships, and duties impact one another's performance. Home care often relies on a community of experts to repair things we cannot, neighbors from whom we borrow a mower, or at least manufacturers who create things we need to keep up our homes. I'm not suggesting that we pursue deep life with all the people I just mentioned; I'm simply noting the fallacy of our worldview. In school, work, home, and lives, we must each look to others at times and ask, "Can you help me?"

I used the term "more confidence than ability" to describe Travis's solo attempt to lift our sofa. The term has come to mind often as I watch my young kids: from Charlotte's first toddle toward the edge of a pool, unaware of the need to swim (we caught her!), to Maggie's first bike ride without training wheels (we caught her too!), young kids attempt so many things they lack the strength and skill for and attempt them with gusto and confidence. In much of life, teens and adults do the same. "I can do it myself," we declare proudly . . . except we can't. We all have more confidence in ourselves than ability.

HOLINESS & LOVE, TOGETHER

Our individualistic mindset impacts our spirituality and flies in the face of the way God made faith, growth, and Christian life. If much of the Christian life is learning to trust God, rely on His Spirit, and obey His commandments, it's impossible to be Christian without living in deep relationship with others!

Today's reading from Colossians references some of the New Testament verses known as the "one another commands." A few actions in Paul's list of "earthly" and "old self" things to "put away" could happen in isolation. But "sexual immorality, impurity, passion, evil desire, and covetousness . . . anger, wrath, malice, slander, . . . obscene talk, . . . lie(s)" are all people-oriented. And in the "new self" life of "God's chosen ones, holy and beloved" *all* the marks Paul lists involve relationship with other humans: "Compassionate hearts, kindness, humility, meekness, and patience" are only on display if another person is involved. Forgiveness, "love," and "perfect harmony" require other people too (often, those toward whom we find it difficult to enact those qualities). We are "one body," "teaching and admonishing one another" (Col. 3:5–16). And I skipped my favorite "one another command": "Bearing with one another," which is also translated, "Be tolerant with one another." (Col. 3:13 GNT). (Even if I cannot fulfill the other commands, surely I can *put up with* fellow believers . . . most of the time!)

Today's reading highlights the interconnectedness between love of God and love of our neighbors as ourselves. These are two sides of one coin; together, they are Jesus' answer when asked about the greatest [single] commandment (Mark 12:28–31). Jesus answers with two commandments that cannot be separated; neither is designed to exist without the other. Rather, says the Son of God, "There is no other commandment greater than these." We display our love of God primarily through our love of neighbor. (Conversely, even some of the most educated people I know who claim to follow Jesus display a *lack of* love for God by a *lack of* love for neighbors.)

There are over one hundred "one another commands" in the New Testament,[6] ranging from "Be at peace with one another," to "Instruct one another," to "Carry each other's burdens," to "Submit to one another," to "Confess your sins to one another"—and lots of "Love one anothers." Our mutual growth into Christian maturity, according to the apostle Paul, happens by "speaking the truth in love"—*with each other*![7] All these "one anothers" are ways to enact Jesus' greatest commandment, to "love your neighbor as yourself," which in turn is a way we worship and "love the Lord [our] God" (12:30–31).

What does Christian love look like? It looks like loving people, created in God's image, with the selfless, sacrificial love of Christ. It looks like pursuing them, even when—not if—they are difficult to love. It looks like living the "one another commands" in God's Word, by the power of God's Spirit. After all, "Whatever you did for . . . the least of these brothers and sisters of mine," Jesus explains, "you did for me" (Matt. 25:40 NIV).

"ONE ANOTHERING"

For The City Church's first decade, our leadership intentionally avoided a centralized "benevolence fund." Rather than members-in-need coming to "the church" (e.g., leadership, the organization), we equipped them to express those needs to their closest communities. We regularly taught our church family concepts like generosity, honesty, sacrifice, care for each other, and "one anothering." So when Nate ran into an expensive medical emergency, our elders did not hear of it until the group leader reported with pride that their group had contributed over $3,000 toward that need. When Jeff and Randi's only car proved to be too small to take everything they needed to their own out-of-town wedding, Sara lent them her brand-new-to-her SUV without question . . . after only a few weeks of having met them! Multiple families in our church prioritize "ministry funds" in their personal budgets, over and above their giving to the church or missions, simply to be generous or meet needs.

Jess and I got to build our house in a neighborhood we felt called on mission to before we had kids. We designed the second level with one bedroom for any future sons and one bedroom for daughters. And we designated a separate bedroom and bathroom with the idea of housing people with various needs. Over the past decade, we've had multiple people live with us, for a month to a year at a time. Some paid rent, others paid nothing, while still others agreed to stipulations to address specific brokenness or discipleship issues they needed to work through.

These examples of neighbor love come from my church family. None are convenient or glamorous; few are comfortable; most will never be known (except on this page). But even in Christian circles, this sacrifice and selfless neighbor love are uncommon. It takes vulnerability to express needs to others in our individualistic society. It takes an "others-focus" to treat our finances and our possessions like this when other common discipleship methods focus on one's private relationship with God above the common good and our mutual need for others. It takes a radical death to self to put others first, in the name of God, when discipleship is typically defined by Sunday church attendance and a few bucks in an offering box.

But the vulnerability to make needs known, the sacrifice to meet those needs, and the engagement of others in decisions like these are ways the people of God display the heart of God in the "one another" commands. The commands I shared above require God's people to "honor one another above yourselves . . . have equal concern for each other . . . serve one another humbly in love . . . carry each other's burdens . . . be kind and compassionate to one another . . . live in harmony with one another . . . offer hospitality to one another without grumbling . . . [and] love one another."[8] In other words, in "one-anothering" people, our love for God is displayed.

A LESSON FROM THE WOODS OF MAINE

Author Michael Finkel tells the true story of a forty-seven-year-old hermit who had lived alone in the Maine woods . . . *for twenty-seven years.*[9] Christopher Knight's motive for this was not religion, protest, or even an escape from society; it was just "to get lost." He even said he had "no plans" when he started; he "just did it." Knight had "no one to tell . . . I didn't have any friends. I had no interest in my co-workers." As he journeyed alone, his story takes a poignant turn: Knight began "to realise that it is almost impossible to live by yourself all the time. You need help."[10]

Finkel's book analyzes hermits, starting in the third century and across the world. Some made and sold goods; others hired themselves out for work. In the eighteenth century, some lived in caves near castles and were paid by aristocrats to appear as a novelty at dinner parties. Knight, however, "wished to be unconditionally alone . . . an uncontacted tribe of one."[11] Even in avoiding people though, Knight was dependent on others: he survived on food and supplies he stole from vacation cabins in the woods.

After over one thousand such break-in's, Knight was finally caught. He reflected, "I lost my identity. There was no audience, no one to perform for. There was no need to define myself. I became irrelevant."[12] In solitude, Knight lost himself. Alone, he became irrelevant. This hermit speaks to a deeper truth than he likely even knows.

101 WAYS TO MOVE FROM FAÇADE TO FAMILY

25 When deciding where to live, find a home with extra space for a guest in need or a spiritual sibling.

26 If you don't think you can afford the previous idea, dive into your finances looking for sacrifices you can make to worship God and serve others.

27 If you have a spare vehicle, or can go without yours, lend it to someone in need.

28 If hiring someone at work, see if a spiritual sibling's skills fit and try to hire them.

Every human is intrinsically relational. Christian or not, we *all* need one another. This is true physically, emotionally, and spiritually. No one is actually self-sufficient; even history's hermits need other people for their sustenance. If this is true for hermits who deeply desire a life apart, how much truer is it for Christians, who are called in Christ to life together? We need deep, meaningful relationships during our lives, and the basis for these "one-anothering" relationships is a deep, meaningful relationship with God.

ANSWER
Your spiritual family involves people who are like and unlike you.

READ
Galatians 3:25–29

SAME KIND OF DIFFERENT . . .

RON HALL WAS A MILLIONAIRE ART DEALER.

Ron met Denver Moore, who had escaped his life of functional slavery in Louisiana in the 1960s, at Fort Worth's Union Gospel Mission. While the common stereotype of this kind of relationship is that Hall was a provider and Moore a receiver, their book (then movie) *Same Kind of Different as Me* displays the two-way relationship these men developed: they learned each other's worldview, were impacted by one another's histories, and shaped each other's faith. They lived together and worked together. And without giving away their story, they carried one another through tragedy. Their story challenges God's people today, who often gravitate toward mono-ethnic, mono-economic, mono-everything faith communities. Moore summarizes his and Hall's early relationship, and in some ways the whole book: "The Word says God don't give us credit for lovin the folks we want to love anyway. No, He gives us credit for loving the unlovable."[13]

WE NEED EACH OTHER'S DIFFERENCES

Like everyone else I know, I gravitate toward people like me. I resonate with people whose personalities, passions, sense of humor, and interests line up with mine. Those relationships are easy. So when I read Hall and Moore's story, the principles confronted my comfort. I have since learned that I grow most, and am most changed, by people in my life who are unlike me. By sharing similar thinking, worldview, and strengths, I also share similar blind spots, gaps, and weaknesses with those like me. My eyes are opened, my assumptions challenged, and my view of God enlarged by others' differences. Today we see that a healthy spiritual family is composed of people who are like us, but also those unlike us.

As I reflect on the various experiences of my church ministry, I often picture the difficulty of deep relationships that existed in history's first church families. From the New Testament letters, we know that slaves and masters had begun following Jesus and were part of the same church families. We know that Jews and Gentiles—whose avoidance of each other stemmed not from mere preference but millennia-long religious law—were now one in Christ. We know that women, who first-century society viewed as second-rate, were valued and played various roles in mission and ministry alongside men. "You are *all* sons of God, through faith" Paul writes to his diverse friends in Galatia (Gal. 3:26). Can you imagine how awkward some interactions must have been? How messy was this new, upside-down, kingdom culture? No one had experienced anything like it! And here's the clincher: no other local church existed where people could go if they didn't like the preacher or if someone offended them.

ETHNICITY: STILL *THE MOST SEGREGATED HOUR*

It's hard to find a divide as distinct in Western churches as that between ethnicities. Martin Luther King Jr.'s words on *Meet the Press* in April 1960 are as true today as when he spoke them: "I think it is one of the tragedies of our nation, one of the shameful tragedies, that 11:00 on a Sunday morning is one of the most segregated hours, if not the most segregated hour, in Christian America. I definitely think the Christian church should be integrated. And any church that stands against integration, and that has a segregated body is standing against the Spirit and stands against the teachings of Jesus Christ, and it fails to be a true witness."[14]

King's strong charge echoes God's Word. Galatians 3 displays a spiritual family that is diverse, integrated, and truly one: Jesus Himself is our peace, "who has made us [all] one and has broken down . . . the dividing wall of hostility" (Eph. 2:14) that existed between Jews and Gentiles (ethnicities), biological sex, slaves and free, and every culture and language. We need the insight that comes from varied ethnicities, to shape our faith and help us more fully understand God.

During the summer of 2020, the world rightly erupted over the death of George Floyd, a black man killed unnecessarily under the unrelenting knee of a white police officer. As a white male nearing my forties, there are elements of grief I cannot fully feel or enter into. But the deep pain in some of my dearest sisters and brothers in Christ breaks my heart. I have listened and learned over several years to understand their hearts and enter into their suffering. I know other white sisters and brothers are seeking the same, and that I have a long way to go. But I also know that my faith is more holistically shaped by knowing the experiences, struggles, views of God, and other elements of faith held by sisters and brothers of color.

Justice, compassion, unity, and reconciliation are concepts that go far deeper than social justice or human rights. These elements—as well as righteous anger, empathy, and godly grief—start with God. Every human is created in God's image, reflecting aspects of their Creator for His glory: "God created man in his own image, in the image of God he created him; male and female he created them" (Gen. 1:27). Our spiritual families are stronger today and foreshadow an eternity of worshiping alongside people from every tribe, tongue, and nation when they are multiethnic.

But experts that promote multiethnic churches say that rather than starting with a staff hire or sermon series, prioritizing multiethnicity starts with individuals and smaller groups, forming meaningful relationships across ethnic divides. In other words, forming this kind of family can start with you. Will our spiritual families break down ethnic dividing walls and lay aside things like comfort, preference, and historical bias for God's glory and everyone's good?

GENDER: UNITY IN DISTINCTION

The first pages of the Bible paint a picture of unity in distinction: Genesis 1 and 2 are a celebration of God and His power, seen through crafting literally everything that exists, out of literally nothing. God's Word describes a world without sin: a perfect world, exactly as God intended it. Light, water, land, every celestial being, every animal on earth, and so forth, came into existence at God's spoken word, over six days, and existed perfectly together for the glory of their Creator. At the end of each of the first five days, God declared His creation "good" (Gen. 1).

But everything in God's creation was not the same as everything else. Birds were distinct from fish; land from water. While each thing God created was immensely valuable and glorified Him, distinctions existed between them. Each glorified Him, not *despite* of their distinctions but *because of,* and *in,* those distinctions. In days one through five of God's creation, unified and distinct things completed each other. And this continued on day six: the pinnacle of this unity in distinction is God creating men and women. We are different, and God does not negate those distinctions. God created us male and female: distinct, unified, and equal. He blessed both genders, then charged both genders to glorify Him, to steward His creation, and to multiply His image. Humans can only do these things when we embrace the distinctions, unity, and equality in which we were created. Like the rest of God's creation, we glorify God when our differences work together.

Modern ministry often separates genders from each other. But my primary relationship to every female follower of Jesus is sister; this is true even of my wife! It would be crazy if I never spoke to my actual sisters and instead only addressed my brothers-in-law. I would be a weaker man and brother if I never had a spiritual conversation with them or asked their advice. Similarly, if the majority of a church's ministry or group's conversations negate the giftings, input, and perspective of the other gender, in some ways, we promote the proverbial "eye [saying] to the hand, 'I have no need of you'" (1 Cor. 12:21).

Yes, some discipleship conversations are best kept gender specific. But in my experience, when we learn to treat others as siblings and help both genders learn to value each other through a lens of healthy, biblical relationship, everyone grows. My wife, Jess, has obviously shaped my life and faith, as have women in my actual family. Nicole, Tina, Erica, Kathy, and Katie are some sisters in Christ who have consistently done so too, alongside female authors and innumerable conversations with women. When we default to pursuing ministry together and bridge the male-female dividing wall Paul describes in today's verses, women and men gain a more holistic perspective of the Bible, shape each other in areas of faith and discipline, and give and receive helpful advice to some confessed sins. When we relegate ministry to one gender or the other, we miss

101 WAYS TO MOVE FROM FAÇADE TO FAMILY

29 Learn what drives your spiritual siblings: fears, motives, goals, passions.

30 Learn stories: How did others grow up, what was their family like, what did (and didn't) they love about their past, and what shaped them?

31 Make comments and ask good questions: draw out the heart's "deep waters."

32 Listen for themes: Where do people find their identity, what do they see as problems and solutions, where is their hope, and what is their "functional savior"?

valuable perspectives and our faith can remain limited. Will we value both genders and pursue mission, ministry and unity in distinction, for God's glory and everyone's good?

A TWO-WAY STREET

Today's examples included socioeconomic, ethnic, and gender dividing walls. These are but three examples among many. I taught interviewing as a class at a local university for five years, and one maxim I shared to prepare students for entering the working world went something like this, "If I hire someone just like me, one of us is irrelevant." Similarly, our churches and groups will be best if they're filled with people unlike each other. Whenever someone marries into a new family, it now includes multiple backgrounds, histories, assumptions, and distinctions. As I've said, we do not choose our literal families, nor is there often good reason to walk out on them. This can be true in our spiritual families too: we accept and appreciate each member as a gift from God, serve and strengthen each other, welcome each other in our weaknesses, and reflect the heart of our one Father as we pursue people who are different and even "unlovable" for our mutual growth. God blesses and shapes us (sometimes in surprising ways!) in this pursuit.

As I've mentioned, my church includes several asylum seekers. Women, children, and men who fled to the US for protection from across the globe. As the US asylum process goes, each is restricted from employment for several years. Ashley and Kurtis had a passion for asylum seekers, which spread to multiple families in our church, and eventually a nonprofit organization was born. At any given moment DASH (dashnetwork.org) now houses over twenty asylum seekers, providing housing, food, friendship, social services, and other necessities. But the asylum seekers provide just as much in return: participants learn about the globe, suffering, family, culture, tradition, commitment, and loss. We learn about each other's faith and grow deeper in knowledge and love of Christ—not despite our differences but because of them.

PAST AND FUTURE GLORY, NOW

This picture is one God paints of our past, present, and future reality. Unity in distinction began with the Trinity, in eternity past. God the Father, God the Spirit, and God the Son are distinct, unified, and equal; they are one God. And in the first pages of the Bible, God was glorified as each unique element of His creation fulfilled the purpose for which God created it, while working with other elements of creation to glorify God together. In the last pages of the Bible, the apostle John gives us a picture of eternity in which all creation is similarly diverse, similarly unified, and similarly glorifying God together.

If this diversity starts with God, and is our past and our future, it should be true of our present church families too. It starts with a single conversation, and with asking God to move you out of your comfort zone. As Ron Hall and Denver Moore attest, there is no limit to what God might do from there. He is glorified as we appreciate peoples' differences and our need for multiple perspectives working in unity. A church family breaks down dividing walls between different things, and stands together as one, for the glory of our three-in-one God.

EVERY GENERATION

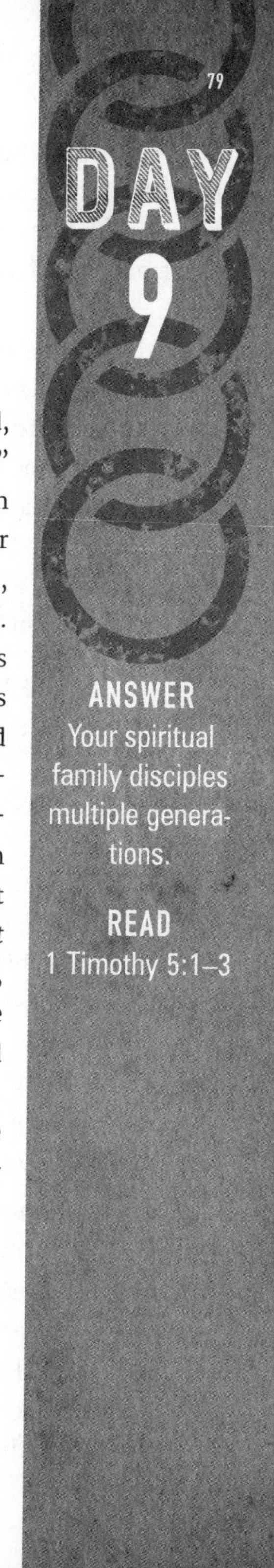

"DADDY, CAN YOU DO A HANDSTAND?"

Maggie, my athletically inclined eight-year-old, asked me during some one-on-one time. "No," I chuckled at the mental image. "Well, I'll teach you," she said confidently. To honor her love for gymnastics and excitement for teaching her dad, I agreed, fully assuming I wouldn't be able to do it. But to my surprise, with God's grace and Maggie's direction, I eventually held a handstand! It was only a few seconds, but I was shocked it happened at all. Maggie was gleeful. I couldn't stop thinking of her exuberant hands-clasped, sparkle-eyed smile, as much for her accomplishment in teaching me than with my actual handstand. But I also kept thinking, *I would* never *have done that on my own*. Maybe it's because I'm pushing forty, have too much on my mind, or lost a child's sense of wonder. Or maybe Maggie and I are just wired differently.

The five people under my roof share the same DNA and spend more time together than nearly any other relationship any of us have. But Charlotte is so different from Maggie, who is so different from Travis, who is so different from me, who is so different from Jess, who is so different from Charlotte. Our personalities are different, we enjoy different hobbies, food, and clothes, our senses of humor and favorite subjects are different, and so forth. At Charlotte's prompting, we even learned recently that, according to J. K. Rowling's *very* official "sorting hat quiz," our whimsical Hogwarts houses would be different. (Two Hufflepuff, two Ravenclaw, and one Gryffindor, for the record.) You get the point.

But each member of my family has shaped me in many ways. Travis's curiosity and his attention to nature's detail and physics help me slow down. Maggie's compassion and feelings have grown mine. Charlotte's joy and logic sharpen my awareness and responses. And Jess's introspection, ability to keep one hundred plates spinning with grace and selfless generosity, and simple but deep spirituality, point me to God, gratitude, and amazement every day. I hope I give to each member of my family half the grace they give to me.

"LET THE CHILDREN COME TO ME"

Throughout His ministry, Jesus used children to teach adults spiritual lessons. Similarly, Old Testament wisdom literature calls children blessings from the Lord. God consistently charges His people to care for vulnerable persons; this includes children and especially orphans.[15]

In both Testaments, parents are charged with the primary discipleship of their children (Prov. 22:6; Eph. 6:4). But interestingly, one of the Bible's most known commands toward children—the famous *shema* in Deuteronomy 6—is given to God's entire covenant community. It's often read through an individualistic lens, assumed to apply only within each nuclear family. But if we apply the stated recipients to each sentence of this passage, it reads,

> "Hear, O *Israel*: The Lord our God, the Lord is one. You [O *Israel*] shall love the Lord your God with all your heart and with all your soul and with all your might. And these words that I command you today shall be on your heart [O *Israel*]. You [O *Israel*] shall teach them diligently to your children, and shall talk of them when you sit in your house, and when you walk by the way, and when you lie down, and when you

rise. You [*O Israel*] shall bind them as a sign on your hand, and they shall be as frontlets between your eyes. You [*O Israel*] shall write them on the doorposts of your house and on your gates." (Deut. 6:4–9)

The consistent direction God gives His people regarding children is inviting them in, including them meaningfully, even learning from them . . . and discipling them together, in the context of committed relationships. Does this sound like most churches' posture toward children today? What about our posture toward the elderly, or widows, or other vulnerable populations? Today we see that a spiritual family is stronger when it involves multiple generations.

A HOUSE DIVIDED . . .

Picture a three-generational family of eight walking into a stereotypical church building on Sunday. (They'd likely be a few minutes late and a little frazzled, but that's just to color the mental picture for you.) Mom and Dad rush their pre-K son and first grade daughter to the check-in desk where a smiling volunteer helps them through the process, then they'd drop each child off with trained professionals who are entrusted with these kids' spiritual development. Their middle school-aged son disappears into a darkened (and hopefully Lysol-ed!) gym with his peers, for games, music, and teaching with another set of trained professionals entrusted with his spiritual development. Grandma and Grandpa take the elevator to the second floor, where other septuagenarians greet them with Folgers coffee, while Mom and Dad go to their own class with other parents of elementary students before the service. They feel a little sad as they take a muffin from the tray; their teacher had told them that since Billy was in middle school now, they'd soon be moved to a new class, one full of strangers to them but designed for parents of teenagers.

This paragraph is a stereotype. But it's not hypothetical; it is the experience of many church buildings today. You've likely experienced a version of it. Having a team of committed people ministering to children *can be* a picture of a whole community, developing of its youngest members. The dangers, though, include entertainment replacing true discipleship as well as parents taking a secondary role in their own child's spirituality to the children's ministry staff and teachers. And to be fair, after their Sunday school classes or small groups, most adults gather in the sanctuary for a multigenerational worship service with intergenerational hugs and greetings. But this one time where generations cross paths does not promote meaningful interactions between members. Everyone looks one direction, and other than singing and maybe praying, the role is largely receiving (teaching, exhortation, prayer, and communion) from the few professionals on the stage.

THE DANGERS OF DIVISION

It might surprise you that this "house divided" practice on Sundays was not the norm for the first 1,970 years or so of following Jesus! For most of history—and still in many parts of the world and in various denominations—the church family is together as one family when they gather. In "A Brief History of Youth Ministry," American youth ministry expert Dave Wright explains that para-church ministries, like Young Life and Youth for Christ, became popular in the mid-1900s. "By the early 70s, churches began to realize the need for specialized ministries to teenagers and began hiring youth pastors. . . . Gatherings with food and live music could draw enormous crowds. Churches found that large, vibrant youth groups drew more families to the church, and, therefore, encouraged more attraction-oriented programs."[16] (Is it coincidental that this sounds like the goals of the church growth movement, which began just before the 1970s?) Wright's article describes youth ministry in the following decades and concludes ominously, "By the start of the 21st century, we discovered many youth were no longer interested in the show that we put on or the oversimplified message. . . . Some youth ministries intensified their effort combining massive hype with strong messages that inspired youth but did not translate to everyday life. We realized we were faced with a generation whose faith was unsustainable."[17]

Research agrees, consistently showing that students leave the church upon graduating from age-specific ministry models. A 2019 LifeWay Research report entitled "Most Teenagers Drop Out of Church as Young Adults" reads in part, "While 69 percent say they were attending at age 17, that fell to 58 percent at age 18 and 40 percent at age 19. Once they reach their 20s, around 1 in 3 say they were attending church regularly. . . . Ben Trueblood, director of student ministry at LifeWay, said those numbers speak to the issue at hand. 'We are seeing teenagers drop out of the church as they make the transition out of high school and student ministry. . . . This moment of transition is often too late to act for churches.'"[18]

Wright offers four reasons for this trend:

> [First] we segregated youth from the rest of the congregation. Students in many churches no longer engaged with "adult" church and had no place to go once they graduated from high school. They did not benefit from intergenerational relationships but instead were relegated to the youth room.
>
> Second, we incorporated an attractional model that morphed into entertainment-driven ministry. In doing that we bought into the fallacy of "edu-tainment" as a legitimate means of communicating the gospel . . .
>
> Third, we lost sight of the Great Commission, deciding instead to make converts of many and disciples of few. We concluded that strong biblical teaching and helping students embrace a robust theology was boring (or only relevant to the exceptionally keen) and proverbially shot ourselves in the foot.
>
> Fourth, we created a consumer mentality amongst a generation that did not expect to be challenged at church in ways similar to what they face at school or on sports teams.[19]

THE GOOD OLD DAYS

While teenage ministry was a case study today, there are dangers in segregating Christians by age. Today's reading from 1 Timothy briefly explains how Christians are to treat people cross-generationally: "Do not rebuke an older man but encourage him as you would a father, younger men as brothers, older women as mothers, younger women as sisters, in all purity. Honor widows who are truly widows" (1 Tim. 5:1–3). These words are familial! They speak of known-ness, love, care, and relationship! How could you treat an actual father, mother, or sibling well if you only saw them in passing while a countdown clock expires and the music leader welcomes the crowd? How can we "encourage" or "honor" people—or, frankly, know them enough to be tempted to "rebuke" them—outside of meaningful relationship?

Day 6's reading from Titus 2 similarly charged older women to "train the young women" and older men to be "a model of good works" and to "urge the younger men" toward holiness (Titus 2:2–7). Both older women and older men are to teach the next generation. That generation is, in turn, to honor and care for the elderly. And as mentioned earlier, the whole church joins together to teach children the ways of the Lord (Deut. 6:7). Throughout the Bible, when God's people gathered, they all did so together—both in smaller pockets and in large gatherings.[20] Entire families were discipled and baptized together.[21] Ministry and mission occurs when many generations bring experiences, strengths, and gifts together for mutual building. As the old African proverb says, "It takes a village to raise a child."

My City Group (the closest relationships in my church) is an intentionally multigenerational group of God's people who know each other increasingly well and live on God's mission together. By inviting university-aged students into intergenerational relationships, they glean from older women's and men's wisdom and experience. They learn overtly spiritual things like biblical knowledge and spiritual maturity. And they observe less-overt-but-still-spiritual things like Christian marriage (and conflict and reconciliation within

Christian marriage), and parenting (with its sanctifying ups and downs). They hear about postcollege work and friendships pursued through the lens of the gospel.

Upon graduating and moving to New York for Alison's acting career, Gabe and Alison told our City Group their marriage was now stronger and that they would be better-prepared parents eventually because of their immersion in the life of our group. The night before Monica and Kesh moved to El Paso for medical school, Monica shared tearfully that she had never experienced people who focused on multigenerational discipleship. Knowing the impact that people in their thirties to sixties had on her, she expressed deep desire to find similar, mutually giving church families for the rest of her life.

Intergenerational, familial churches don't just benefit the younger generation. As a married guy with young kids, I am consistently shaped by Rodger and Carol, group members in their sixties. Their matter-of-factness and decades of learning "not to sweat the

101 WAYS TO MOVE FROM FAÇADE TO FAMILY

33 Teach each other's kids: if a child in your spiritual family struggles with math and you're good with numbers, help tutor.

34 Engage each other's kids: involve children in conversations. Get to know them appropriately. Come alongside parents in valuing them.

35 Train each other's kids: give kids a chance to pray or share the gospel, for example, and help parents train their kids how.

36 Discipline each other's kids: a true family even joins parents in correcting each other's kids. Agree on standards, then treat each other's kids as your own.

small stuff" have served my family. Similarly, I glean from and encourage confidence in Mike, who in his sixties still considers himself new to faith and is one of the most godly men I know, and Mary, one of the most joyful, peaceful, and prayerful people I've ever met. Mike and Mary, and Rodger and Carol similarly express what an encouragement "you kids are," as they see an earnestness and commitment to each other (and to the "old fogies" too) among group members who are half their age. Like my daughter Maggie teaching me handstands, younger Christians can impact older, just as much as older can train the younger. Our spiritual families are stronger when they cross generations.

WEEK TWO IN ACTION

The last day of each week you will read how churches across the world live as a family and will discuss this week's content with others. As you discuss the questions, be honest with yourself and others, and let them speak truth in love as you put this book into practice together.

LIVING AS FAMILY: INNER WEST CHURCH, MELBOURNE, AUSTRALIA

I think one of the most beautiful experiences of our church living as a family came through the roller coaster of life in 2020's COVID pandemic. Various Australian lockdown restrictions meant that both our church and our missional communities spent most of 2020 meeting online. So we were forced to learn to serve one another primarily through listening and through prayer. But God bore such fruit from this!

One of our members who already finds maintaining relationships quite difficult really struggled with having to get together over Zoom and unfortunately dropped off the map mid-2020. Eight months on, the members of our missional community family are still praying for him regularly, seeking God's help and leading in how we can serve him, and praying that we would be able to have him rejoin us at the table.

This has really given me such a wonderful insight into who we are as the family of God. It is a bond that is fixed in Christ. Someone who is your brother, sister, aunt, uncle, father or mother by blood will always be that to you, irrespective of what happens relationally. Similarly, in light of what God's done, we are family, irrespective of who we are or how well we're doing. Our missional community family's capacity to continually and committedly hold space for this guy has been such a grace to witness.

One of our other missional community family's members lost both his father and his mother-in-law during the harshest lockdown restrictions. The restrictions meant that we couldn't be physically present to love and comfort him and his family, but as a missional community family, we committed ourselves to daily prayer for their family, as well as sending flowers and food when we could.

The pandemic also drove our everyday lives to be far more localized than ever before. Our missional community family took the opportunity the pandemic gave us to go for walks together at the same time each week, and to the same places, having our kids play at the same parks. The joy of this was learning that "quality time" often happens in the context of "quantity time." We got to know

101 WAYS TO MOVE FROM FAÇADE TO FAMILY

37 Serve parents: help parents see blind spots in their kids' lives and their parenting. (Be prayerful, loving, careful, bold, and humble.)

38 Engage each other's kids: involve children in conversations. Get to know them appropriately. Come alongside parents in valuing them.

39 Prioritize time with older saints too: these beautiful, cross-generational, two-way relationships lead to gleaning, living, and learning together.

40 Prioritize fewer people: This sounds harsh, but intentional relationships with fewer people are better than surface relationships with more.

each other's hearts more deeply and speak the gospel more sharply whilst also having the opportunity to draw neighbors and friends into that dynamic too!

Some of the households in our missional community have been intentionally loving and serving a local family that moved to the neighborhood two years ago. They are not Christians and moved into the neighborhood having just migrated from Europe! The first three families they met in Australia were all Christians, who gave themselves to loving them and sharing the gospel with them in word and deed. We sadly saw them off as they moved interstate, but we are grateful to have been able to share our lives together, and are praying that God will keep revealing himself to them through His people wherever they are.

Jon Tran

"WHO" QUESTIONS TO DISCUSS

- ☐ **GENERAL**: What impacted you most this week? What was new, convicting, difficult, or confusing? What biblical truths do you need others to remind you of in love?
- ☐ **GENERAL**: What about this week reminded you of your church experience, and what was different from your experience with churches? In what ways is that both good and hard?
- ☐ **DAY 6**: What is freeing about knowing you don't have to, and likely cannot, pursue the depth of relationship God calls us to with more than fifteen people? What's hard about that?
- ☐ **DAY 6**: Why do you think so much spiritual fruit comes in smaller groups of committed believers discipling each other? What would it take for you to commit to such a group?
- ☐ **DAY 7**: Why do you think many Christians try to "do it myself" in the Christian life? How are you fighting individualism and seeking "one another" relationships?

- [ ] **DAY 7**: In what ways can Christian growth, fruit, and discipleship only be seen among committed relationships? In what ways have you experienced this?

- [ ] **DAY 8**: How much diversity (gender, age, ethnicity, socioeconomic, etc.) exists in your close spiritual family? What gospel promises and benefits does diversity bring to the family of God?

- [ ] **DAY 8**: What "dividing walls" make your close spiritual family more "mono-" than "multi-" and in what ways can you model Jesus' heart and pursue unity with people "unlike" you?

- [ ] **DAY 9**: How does your close spiritual family value children? How are kids included and cared for like family, and how are they excluded or divided? Why?

- [ ] **DAY 9**: How does your spiritual family value people of multiple generations and the mutual upbuilding and different types of discipleship that occurs in a multigenerational family?

- [ ] **GENERAL**: Look over this week's "101 Ways." What else could you do, per your own gifting, spiritual family, and mission field, to live as God's family? Post ideas with the hashtag, #genuine community.

WEEK THREE

WHAT DOES A SPIRITUAL FAMILY DO?

WHAT DO YOU DO WITH PEOPLE YOU LOVE?

When I ask this question to groups during training events about "everyday mission" or "everyday discipleship," initial responses come easily: "Watch movies," "Eat together," "Give gifts," "Celebrate _____ [insert holiday or milestone here]," and sometimes even "Vacation together." Before long, the initial responses give way to a couple deeper answers: "We want the best for them," one woman may respond. A man might follow, "We take care of them." After a few more responses, a woman in the back says softly, "We forgive them." "Oof, yah," another comments, "even if it's hard—like, if they really hurt us—if we love them, we try to heal those wounds."

For two weeks we have learned about spiritual and theological motivations—our hearts and our minds, our theology and our history—around the deep relationships of a spiritual family. The rest of the book is more tangible. Good theology and right motivation are good starting points, but as Jesus' own half brother asked, "What good is it, my brothers, if someone says he has faith but does not have works?" (James 2:14). James's assumed answer is that it's no good! He continues, "So also faith by itself, if it does not have works, is dead. But someone will say,

'You have faith and I have works.' Show me your faith apart from your works, and I will show you my faith by my works" (2:17–18).

Starting this week, we consider how we can actually live a devoted life together in God's spiritual family. Week Three asks, "What does a spiritual family do?" How do we relate, as spiritual siblings in devoted relationships? How do we put belief into practice? What are practical ways we can pursue the devoted discipleship and mutual benefit that the Bible describes?

Believing the Bible's teaching about committed Christian relationship is good, but the rest of this book invites us to turn that faith into action. By the Spirit's power and for God's glory, we look at showing our faith by our works. So say a prayer as we dive into Week Three, answering the question, "What Does a Spiritual Family Do"?

FIRST STEPS

MY PARENTS DO NOT CELEBRATE THEMSELVES WELL.

My dad and mom are the most consistently selfless people I know. They both turned sixty-five during the COVID-19 pandemic, and my sisters and I decided it was time they heard how their lives had impacted others. You may recall that during the pandemic, the videoconferencing platform "Zoom" became a household term. So we surprised my parents with a combined Zoom birthday party. A few minutes into the seemingly informal call "just to wish dad 'Happy 65th'" (his came first), several other couples were suddenly admitted, who then shared toasts and affirmations. Many were decades in the making. My parents were shocked. They were in the spotlight for a rare moment, receiving affirmation and gratitude.

Maybe you are encouraged often. Many people—especially those who pour themselves out for others—generally find their efforts to be thankless. Selfless people are not "in it" for accolades. But a lack of encouragement opposes biblical principles: "Outdo one another in showing honor," and "Encourage one another and build one another up," Paul writes (Rom. 12:10; 1 Thess. 5:11). My friend Elliot Grudem, who pastors many pastors, summarizes Hebrews 3:13 poignantly, "Without encouragement people die."

Most Christians know encouragement is biblical and needed. But we rarely make time for it. One man I know quipped after toasts at his retirement party, "That was beautiful to hear on my last day, but I would have loved to know how they thought of me while we worked together!" Similarly, I realized a couple years ago that I'd think appreciative thoughts or mention to Jess something I liked that someone did or said but seldom thanked the person! I've tried to combat this with texts or calls when encouraging or grateful thoughts cross my mind. (I've even scrounged for a stamp and written an old-fashioned note!) If "encourage one another" is a biblical command, what would it look like if we actually obeyed it?

BABY STEPS

Day 7 introduced the biblical theology of the "one another" commands and said the New Testament lists one hundred of them. In today's Scripture passage, Peter mentioned some of them. A theology of "one another-ing" is helpful, similar to a house needing a solid foundation. But it becomes livable only with insulation, plumbing, wiring, and Sheetrock. So today looks at tangibly following some "one another" commands in our life together.

Let's start by guarding against anxiety: any new practice takes, well, *practice*. Like a toddler learning to walk, small first steps into "one another-ing" are worth celebrating. But toddlers keep practicing. Let's also remember our commitment to our close spiritual family and see them as a grace-filled venue for practicing these commands. We can't become experts at obeying one hundred commands with every Christian we know overnight. As we consider these commands, let's start by practicing a few, alongside a few committed people.

PICK SIX

In 1 Peter 3, we find six ways Jesus' followers relate to one another. Each phrase below is intrinsically relational, penned under

God's inspiration by Peter, whom Jesus commanded thrice, "Feed my sheep" (John 21:15–17). Here are brief glimpses of living out these six commands, examples among the other ninety-four.

1. *"Have unity of mind"* (1 Peter 3:8)

"Unity" is a common theme of the "one another" commands. More than "getting along," Christian unity exists when things that are different come together for God's glory. In Romans 14, Paul encourages this unity, rather than dividing over differences or asking others to ignore their conviction. Some people in Rome's first church avoided certain meats while others did not. Some chose to celebrate cultural feasts and holidays; others did not. Differing opinions exist in churches today on things like politics and parenting, education and justice. (And the debate over meat continues today too!) To both sides of the "meat divide," Paul writes, "Let not the one who eats despise the one who abstains, and let not the one who abstains pass judgment on the one who eats, for God has welcomed him" (Rom. 14:3). He points to heart motive rather than outward action: "The one who observes the day, observes it in honor of the Lord. The one who eats, eats in honor of the Lord, since he gives thanks to God, while the one who abstains, abstains in honor of the Lord and gives thanks to God" (14:6).

Christian unity occurs when different sides come together, even celebrating each other's convictions in our shared pursuit of honoring God. People in my church pursue this when perspectives differ; for example, trying to interact personally and with love when discussing politics, when the cultural expectation is to destroy each other from afar. As we'll see later, the Bible commands us to rebuke, teach, and "one another." But we start by showing grace, giving the benefit of the doubt, and hearing each other's perspectives. A primary goal in engaging each other's differences is to pursue and celebrate one another's shared motive, which must first be the glory of God.

2. *"[Have] sympathy"* (1 Peter 3:8)

"Sympathy," while widely used, is not always well understood or encouraged. At times, sympathy is harder than empathy; it's easier to "rejoice with those who rejoice, weep with those who weep" if I've experienced similar loss as the weeping sister or felt similar feelings as the rejoicing brother (Rom. 12:15). Sympathy may take more work, because it means caring even if we lack shared experience or understanding! Sympathy enacts deep care, wise comfort, and even heartfelt commiseration for others, even if we don't fully "get it."

In the Old Testament book of Job, the suffering protagonist calls his friends "miserable comforters" because they tried to theologize, logicize, and inform Job's brain in the midst of his heart- and soul-level suffering (Job 16:2). But what's often missed in Job's friends is their first actions, which were beautifully compassionate: "They raised their voices and wept, and they tore their robes and sprinkled dust on their heads toward heaven. And they sat with him on the ground seven days and seven nights, and no one spoke a word to him." Job's friends wanted "to show him sympathy and comfort him," and they did so best before saying a word (Job 2:11–13)! City Church leaders refer to Job's friends when we equip church members for hospital visits or to enter their friends' pain. Sitting in silence and asking questions are skills many lack; we want to "fix it" and give advice. But learning each other's perspectives, and simply weeping or staying silent—even if we don't fully understand—is living out Christian sympathy together.

3–5. *"[Have] brotherly love, [have] a tender heart, and [have] a humble mind"* (1 Peter 3:8)

These commands are distinct but intertwined. "Brotherly love" is a deep affection and pursuit of another's well-being equaling our pursuit of our own. In Genesis 4, Cain murdered his brother Abel. He is cursed, in part, for his hate toward his brother. Instead of being his "brother's keeper," Cain was his brother's destroyer (Gen. 4:9). "Brotherly love" for our siblings in Christ stems from Cain's greatest foil. Jesus, our own "eldest brother" displayed "greater love . . . that someone lay down his life for his friends" (John 15:13).

Second, humility is "count[ing] others more significant than yourselves." Jesus modeled this on our behalf, "taking the form of a servant [and] becoming obedient to the point of death, even death on a cross" (Phil. 2:3, 7–8). Third, pastor and author Ray Ortland defines tender-heartedness as deeper than "not willingly caus[ing] pain," and being "eager to relieve it." My friend Ben Fort reflected on this concept, "Widespread, this would change our responses to racism, sexism, and the burden of singlehood," among other areas of deep personal hurt. This, too, reflects Jesus' heart, Ortlund states, calling Christians "beyond letter-of-the-law compliance with minimal biblical requirements. It goes all the way, where the grace of the gospel sets a new tone."[1]

As God's Spirit produces fruit in us, our pursuit of love, tender-heartedness, and humility start with Jesus' examples. Our worshipful obedience might start as simply as taking a deep breath and considering our words before we respond or react to someone whose view differs from ours, especially on hot-button issues (and on social media). This itself displays grace!

6. "Do not repay evil for evil or reviling for reviling, but on the contrary, bless, for to this you were called." (1 Peter 3:9)

The two sides of "one another-ing" in this verse are entwined like the previous three in verse 8. Jesus was "despised and rejected" (Isa. 53:3); "When he was reviled, he did not revile in return; when he suffered, he did not threaten, but continued entrusting himself to him who judges justly" (1 Peter 2:23). Relying on Christ's gospel and the Spirit to motivate actions they couldn't naturally conjure up, first-century Christians followed Jesus' example and displayed their belief that vengeance is God's to enact, not their own (Rom. 12:19). They turned the other cheek as government officials and religious leaders sought their death (Matt. 5:39). They displayed toward their persecutors the mercy and grace God first showed themselves in Christ.

Suffering and community are related, as seen throughout 1 Peter and the New Testament. Some of the most overt times in history when Christians realize our need for others' encouragement, exhortation, and help doing good have occurred while suffering for Jesus' name. Perseverance, endurance, and consistency are hard when faced alone, but story after story prove that Christians suffer better when we suffer together. We need one another to turn us from our natural responses of evil and reviling and help us "count it all joy, my brothers, when you meet trials of various kinds" (James 1:2).

THE NEXT CHAPTER

Again, the above commands are only six of the dozens in the Bible. If you feel that by God's grace you live those specific commands well or if you want to practice others, today's passages included three more commands in Peter's next chapter: "Keep loving one another earnestly, since love covers a multitude of sins," "Show hospitality to one another without grumbling," and "As each has received a gift, use it to serve one another, as good stewards of God's

101 WAYS TO MOVE FROM FAÇADE TO FAMILY

41 Share your story, so your spiritual siblings can know you better. (Appendix A helps you.)

42 Create a culture of sharing stories often—listen for God's promises, biblical truths, and areas of unbelief in each other's stories (again, see Appendix A.)

43 Respond to stories with biblical truth: speak true identity, gospel promise, and hope in Christ.

44 Point to Jesus as the hero of every question, pain, struggle, sin, and longing of others' stories.

varied grace" (1 Peter 4:8–10). Or choose any other "one another" command: "One third of the one-another commands deal with the unity of the church. . . . One third . . . instruct Christians to love one another. . . . 15% stress an attitude of humility and deference among believers," and there are others.[2] There is no "right" starting point for displaying God's heart toward "one another." But one thing God's family does is actively, prayerfully grow in these practices.

EACH OTHER'S STORIES

A tangible action that helps us is learning each other's stories. It's impossible to love someone without knowing them. This is true with God and our spouse; with literal family members and with our spiritual siblings. We cannot settle for knowing *about* others; we have to truly *know* them to love them well. Paying attention to each other's stories and listening to each other through the lens of God's objective, true story lays a foundation for deep known-ness and true, biblical love. The better we understand each other's passions, upbringings, struggles, gifts, families, and even seemingly mundane aspects of each other's daily lives, the easier it is to form a bond of siblinghood together. The more we know each other's lives, the more likely we are to interact with grace and deference. Since "sharing your story" can be vague, Appendix A includes time-tested templates for sharing stories through a spiritual lens, in a way that highlights helpful aspects of each other's lives.

As we close today's reading, I want to free you and challenge you to obey God, together: choose a "one another" command, pray for God's power, and practice! Living out God's commands with one another is a first answer to the question, "What does a spiritual family do?"

DAY 12

GROWING UP TOGETHER

ANSWER
A spiritual family "speak[s] the truth in love" together.

READ
Ephesians 4:1–16

"HOW DO WE GROW IN CHRISTIAN MATURITY?"

I've asked that question during dozens of discipleship trainings across North America. Every time it gets two immediate responses—"read the Bible" and "pray"—then silence. Sometimes more answers come, but these are the autoreply to growing in Christ. Yes, increasingly knowing and obeying God through reading His Word and communing with Him in regular prayer are vital for Christian life. But today's text from Ephesians shows us why those activities alone are insufficient for His children's growth: a spiritual family must "speak the truth in love" together.

Ephesians 4 charges Christians to unity and deep relationships (vv.1–6), then explains two gifts God gives to achieve that unity: first "grace . . . according to the measure of Christ's gift" (v.7), then others: variously gifted people, each strong in some aspects of faith and weak in others. "He gave the apostles, the prophets, the evangelists, the shepherds and teachers, to equip the saints for the work of ministry, *for building up the body of Christ*" (vv.11–12).

No matter how "mature" we are, only Christ perfectly embodied every spiritual gift. Jesus is the perfect "sent one" (apostle) who entered darkness to start and sustain a globe-changing movement. Jesus is the perfect prophet, incarnating God's Word on earth, and the perfect evangelist, the pinnacle of God's good news who calls people to Himself through His Spirit. Jesus is our Chief Shepherd, who perfectly cares for every sheep, and our perfect Teacher, the very truth of God in word and deed. Since God designed humans in His image, and since each follower of Jesus is His spiritual offspring, we reflect some of our Father's DNA. God gives some people apostolic giftings (the original Twelve, and others in the New Testament and today). He made some people prophetic (whether they carried the title or not). He wired some more evangelistic and others more shepherding. And he gave some daughters and sons the gift of teaching. We each need each other's giftings to become mature in Christ; together we reflect his completeness.

GROWING IN CHRIST, TOGETHER

Paul guards readers against three common but insufficient ways we try to grow into maturity: "Every wind of doctrine, by human cunning, by craftiness in deceitful schemes." Our reliance on these concepts alone, Paul says, leaves us as "children" (the opposite of "maturity"), "tossed to and fro by the waves" (Eph. 4:14). Here's what he means:

Maturity Takes More Than Knowledge

"Every wind of doctrine" acknowledges our need to know God deeply, while guarding us against defining maturity by the amount of Bible and theology we absorb. Knowledge alone "puffs up," and cannot produce true growth (1 Cor. 8:1). Some Doctors of Theology have memorized much of the Bible, but are far from God. I grew up in a religious culture and was hired as a minister at age eighteen. I'm increasingly convinced I did not truly know Jesus until two years into that job. (This is not the ideal order for those events!) I could teach teenagers the Bible, saw kids meet God, and knew *about* Jesus—but did not actually, personally *know* Jesus! God redeemed me, but that experience haunts me for religious people today: Do we fill our heads with knowledge but miss Jesus' work in our hearts?

Jesus claimed that the Pharisees (the most religious people of his day) meticulously knew the Law (doctrine) but consistently missed God's heart. His warning: "You search the Scriptures because you think that in them you have eternal life; and it is they that bear witness about me, yet you refuse to come to me that you may have life" (John 5:39–40). The Bible is consistent: head knowledge is important, but insufficient to produce true heart change and lasting Christian maturity.

Maturity Takes More Than Ability

"Human cunning" is one's ability to figure things out and rely on one's own skill. "Cunning" has negative connotations today of slyness and manipulation. But like "shrewdness," historically "cunning" simply implied cleverness and intelligence. In this light, we cannot be surprised that some first-century Christians relied on their intelligence and abilities to try to grow in godliness . . . because some twenty-first-century Christians do the same! From "five easy steps . . ." sermons to "twenty minutes of [some spiritual activity] each day"; from filling our calendars with Christian activity, to reading books or engaging issues that reflect "Judeo-Christian values," many Christians believe our faith rises or falls proportionately with the number of things we do for God, or avoid, in His name.

The Christian life engages thought, word, and deed; as the previous point acknowledged the Bible as vital, so will our actions and desires increasingly grow in godliness. Even Jesus' half brother calls us to "be doers of the word, and not hearers only, deceiving yourselves" (James 1:22). But our attempts to obey God, fight sin, and pursue holiness by our own power are insufficient. No amount of church attendance, activity, or rules we make can produce Christian maturity.

I recall putting rules on dating relationships during that season I was a minister but not yet a Christian. "No movies in the bedroom alone with my date," was Rule #1 (*Bad things only happen in bedrooms*, was my childish thought). But the mere act of moving to a couch made that rule an insufficient temptation-blocker. So on came, Rule #2: "No reclining more than 45 degrees on the couch" (apparently nothing bad could happen at 44 degrees, while all was lost at 46). I'm mocking my former self, but the problem with "human cunning" is that *we're just too cunning*! We find ways to bend rules, or to go right through them. "The heart is deceitful above all things," Jeremiah tells us (Jer. 17:9). While discipline, routine, and Christian activity are helpful, we cannot rely on our abilities to produce true maturity.

Maturity Takes More Than a Method

A final common, but insufficient, way Paul guards us from trying to grow in Christ is pursuing "craftiness in deceitful schemes (Eph. 4:14)." While "cunning" is more neutral than we assume, "craftiness" and "deceit" are just plain negative. But many Christians pursue "schemes" that make us feel like we're growing in godliness. Some televangelists promise blessing if viewers donate, and some publishers prioritize sales over biblical truth. Spiritual versions of "get-rich-quick scams" promise sin's defeat, and preachers guarantee growth if congregants devote themselves to specific practices. Deceitful craftiness fills our churches and minds: It's subtle, because temptation has been subtle since the serpent's lie in Genesis 3. And it promises holiness, blessing, and freedom—it is enticing, but it always comes up short.

The great deceiver—who has lured people from God since the garden of Eden—still convinces us that these three insufficient methods to grow in Christ work. Following his pattern with Adam and Eve, we start doubting God's goodness and promises if we find an area of life that isn't as mature as we'd like it to be. We pursue a quick fix—perhaps a book or podcast. (How many times have you explained a struggle and received the seemingly exclusive prescription, "Have you read [some book]?" or "I heard this great sermon by [popular pastor]"?) We think we can fix ourselves using our knowledge, our ability, or some method. Like Adam and Eve, the promised result may be enticing, but actually leads us away from God: we place our hope in something other than Christ, to produce "Christian growth."

FROM CHILDHOOD TO MATURITY

These insufficient methods of growing in Christ pervade Christian minds and churches. They initially feel like they work. But like a child getting full on candy, we need better, lasting nourishment. Why is each of these appealing? Because each puts the focus on *ME*! Knowledge bases maturity on *my mind*; cunning bases it on *my ability*; schemes base it on *my (or someone else's) method*. Our individualistic minds love it: "I can produce my fruit, growth, and maturity." It sounds great . . . but God tells me I am a poor redeemer. We cannot be our own saviors.

Paul then points to the one thing that does produce fruit, growth, and maturity in areas we're weak: reliance on God and other Christians. "Rather [e.g., instead of those other, false and fading methods], *speaking the truth in love*, we are to grow up in every way into him who is the head, into Christ" (Eph. 4:15). "Speaking the truth" doesn't mean throwing Bible verses at each other. Paul explains, "The truth is in Jesus" (4:21). The one true way we grow in maturity is our spiritual siblings helping us remember how God's perfect truth, ability, and ways change our lives; how His story (which we say we build our lives on) is actually better than other stories we believe in given moments or situations. We all struggle to believe, remember, and trust God at times. We're each weak in some ways. We're each underdeveloped in areas of faith and life. God grows us by reminding us how His good news impacts every aspect of our lives—and He uses other Christians to deliver those reminders.

Together, my City Group often acknowledges our weaknesses and difficulties applying God's truth to various situations. Then our spiritual siblings lovingly help each other remember and apply God's truth. I felt guilty and responsible when a group member walked away from Christian obedience. Gabe (a group member) gently reminded me that God's care and pursuit of the former member surpassed mine and that God alone turns peoples' hearts. Separately, during a discussion on the image of God, one group meeting devolved into a politically charged debate over human rights. Bob had to rebuke Gerald for an insensitive comment Gerald made about Erik's deeply held convictions, but Bob's rebuke came with love and a history of deep relationship.[3] The meeting ended with greater understanding of different perspectives, repentance and forgiveness, and a long, unified prayer between Gerald and Erik, whose viewpoints still differed from each other. We all grew a little more into Christ that night as we do each time "truth in love" is spoken into everyday situations.

"YOU COMPLETE ME"

Every Christian needs "truth in love" to help us grow; we need others' experiences and gifts to offset areas we are less mature and less gifted in. "You complete me" was an impassioned plea to Dorothy Boyd (Renée Zellweger) in the 1996 film *Jerry Maguire* (Tom Cruise). The line has been well-quoted since. (So has Boyd's response, "You had me at hello.")[4] While cheesy, the words are true in a close spiritual family. While my relationship with God is personal, it is not individualistic. God gave us the gift of each other, so that "*we all* attain to the unity of the faith and of the knowledge of the Son of God [together], to mature manhood [together], to the measure of the stature of the fullness of Christ [together]" (Eph. 4:13).

When Paul says we "grow up *in every way*" into Christ (v. 15), we realize we can't view maturity like a line graph that steadily moves up and to the right. Despite common vernacular in church circles, we can't say, "she's mature" or "he's immature" as across-the-board definitions, like "she's a teenager" or "he's middle-aged." Instead, Christian maturity is more like a bar graph: mine might show 60 percent maturity in "teaching" gifts, 42 percent in "humility," and 80 percent in "faith." It might show only 30 percent in "shepherding" giftings, but by God's grace, that's up from 22 percent a decade ago, as I've learned from better shepherds. Some areas of my faith and gifting would rank higher and other areas lower.

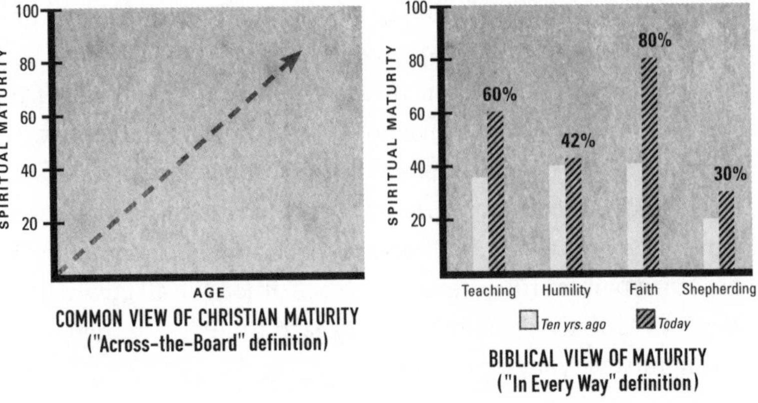

This is a silly (and nerdy!) picture of maturity, but honest assessments show this to be true of us all: by God's grace, we're each gifted—more "mature"—in *some ways*, and we're each less gifted—less "mature"—in *other ways*. We need each other to grow up *in every way*! I'm more compassionate today because of Chris, Sawyer, Camp, and Kathy—all neighbors, fellow church members, and gifted shepherds. I am more prayerful and faith-filled because of Mike and Mary.

45 Update each other: find a group app and share joys, burdens (even silly moments and questions) together.

46 Exhort one another: don't keep biblical truth, God's promises, or thoughts on applying the gospel to life to yourself!

47 Encourage one another: intentionally affirm growth and celebrate fruit in others.

48 Point to Jesus: respond to updates, requests, needs, or struggles by pointing to God and truths that apply to each scenario.

I am better equipped for biblical justice because of Shaun, Alex, Tina, Kesh, Monica, and Nicole. And I hope that each of those women and men is "more mature" in some way because they've gleaned from my gifting too.

As the family of God, we must speak God's truth into each other's life, as we grow into maturity together. As we become confident in God, understand His truth more, trust His Spirit in us, and increasingly accept the ways He's gifted us for others, we can "speak truth in love" together and help others grow in areas that God has gifted us that others need. God's grace is the first gift Paul tells the Ephesians God gives: Christ alone unifies His body, rather than letting us exist as individuals, or some members rejecting each other and remaining weaker. And it's through God's second gift—each member of Christ's body working as one, helping each other grow up in every way—that "the body grow[s] so that it builds itself up in love" (4:16).

ANSWER
A spiritual family is inconvenienced for each other.

READ
Acts 4:32–37

MI CASA ES SU CASA

"FRIENDS HELP EACH OTHER. YES THEY DO, IT'S TRUE."[5]

Those lyrics came from a child's TV show as I tried to find the right words to start today's reading. They're from PBS's preschool-aimed *Daniel Tiger's Neighborhood*, an offshoot of *Mister Rogers' Neighborhood*. The annoyingly catchy melody distracted me from finding the perfect introduction. Just before I asked them to turn the music down, I realized it exactly reflects today's verses from Acts 4. A spiritual family "help[s] each other. Yes they do, it's true."

Except that while the kids' song sounds nice, it is not most adults' experience. Rather, most adults can resonate with: "Friends say nice things to each other. Yes they do, it's true." Or "Christian friends offer to pray for each other. And sometimes they actually do, it's true." We serve someone if the "cost-benefit ratio" feels in balance. But are we deeply, truly "friends [who] help each other"? Or would we admit to Mr. Roger's make-believe friend, "No we don't, it's false"?

Many songs, for both adults and children, promote togetherness, standing up for others, and sacrificial service.[6] Charts across musical styles echo lessons kids learned from *Sesame Street*, *Barney and Friends*, or *Doc McStuffins* (depending on the decade): helping others is good. Jesus "came not to be served but to serve, and to give his life as a ransom for many" (Matt. 20:28). He "[laid] down his life for his friends" (John 15:13). If we follow Jesus, shouldn't we live as He lived and obey God as He obeyed? Today looks at laying down our own lives—putting aside our preferences and comfort—for others' sake. Because spiritual families are inconvenienced for each other.

WHAT'S MINE IS YOURS

The Spanish phrase "Mi casa es su casa" captures the heart of Acts 4: "No one said that any of the things that belonged to him was his own, but they had everything in common" (v. 32). The closest English phrase might be "make yourself at home." That's how God's early church saw their homes, finances, possessions, and food: as from God, to steward well for God's purposes. A decade ago, it would have been hard for me to fathom twenty-first-century Americans living so counterculture to our individualistic, capitalist society. But in my church and others, I've now seen this same communal devotion in action.

In our local church, Karl and Susan, empty nesters with spare rooms, invited an asylum seeker and her three children into their home; for ten months they lived as family, sharing meals, chores, stories, faith, and life. Jimmy and Jamey regularly hire people experiencing homelessness for their remodeling company, giving them responsibility, paid work, and treating them with dignity. My own family hardly had to buy newborn clothes for our son Travis—Sally, Christine, and Julie passed down clothes for the first boy in the Connelly Casa.

Looking outside of our local church's weekly gatherings, San Francisco's We Are Church is intentionally held in zero-rent spaces (like homes), and they avoid paid staff in their churches (their pastors work other jobs), so 100 percent of giving goes to help others and support mission. And the Tampa Underground Network sees "microchurches" form around mission to all sorts of people groups and needs. The people involved in each of these small missional communities are committed to use their resources to bless each other and those they're on mission for.

Depending on one's culture, wedding showers help couples get items for their life together, or families add a room or wing onto their communal home for the new couple. In many churches, people similarly give new or expectant parents gifts for new babies, then provide a few weeks' meals once the baby arrives. Some of these efforts are cultural norms, but what if Christians always lived like this? Could we use our God-given homes, finances, possessions, meals, and resources not just for ourselves, but for "each as any had need" (v. 35)?

SACRIFICE FOR OTHERS

A mark of a servant is a willingness to be inconvenienced for someone else's convenience. We can reflect Jesus' ultimate sacrifice for our ultimate good, even in small ways, as we choose to "deny [ourselves] and take up [our] cross daily and follow me" (Luke 9:23). We can serve our spiritual families in many ways, which require inconvenience and sacrifice. But here are three biblical ways we can model God's selfless heart together.

1. Messy Hospitality

Hospitality, at its core, is meaningfully including someone who doesn't belong. It can take two forms, which both require sacrifice. First, hospitality means bringing people into our homes.[7] Beyond formal events or planned meetings—and even without the chance to clean our bathrooms first!—it means letting people into the realities of our messy lives. I don't know how many people have keys to my house. Tyler and Bethany crashed there last minute while my family was out of town. Neighbors help themselves to baking ingredients or lawn care supplies. We were out once, and the dryer buzzed while Julie was there dropping something off. She folded our laundry, and also did some light cleaning, before we got home! That may seem invasive, but it's a glimpse of a deep, caring relationship.

If one form of hospitality is inviting others into our lives and messiness, a second sacrificial form involves leaving our comfort zones and going into others' lives and messiness. When we began fostering children, we were unaware of Texas's standards for who can babysit foster kids. Caregivers must be background checked and certified in first aid, CPR, and other safety processes. (This is reasonable, for the record; we were simply new to the process and unaware.) A married couple in our close spiritual family, as well as a single man and a single woman, became certified just to come alongside my family in caring for these kids! That was an unexpected display of joining us in our passion. They laid aside their norms and came onto our turf, for our good. Giving up comfort, privacy, and time for others' good is sacrificial service.

2. Consider the Communal Impact

Some of our friends have lived in New York City for five years. Even though Alison is "making it" in the uber-competitive theater scene there, they are considering moving away. But while logic, and maybe financial prudence, would automatically lead many people to an immediate decision, they were hesitant because of the strong community they made over those years and told me how "it hurts our church family to see people come and go." Considering the impact a potential departure would have on others is an example of prioritizing the common good.

Any consideration of communal welfare in one's personal decisions is a sacrifice. Matt declined a job with a longer commute to make more time for others—even though it paid more than the job he took. Tyler and Bethany, who crashed at our house last-minute, did so because they had returned from years of overseas mission work. Rather than starting afresh in a new city, they wanted to recommit to the spiritual family they had left. So they limited their job and house searches. Giving up career advancement, finances, and desire is sacrificial service.

3. Restorative Discipline

A third way we sacrifice for others is laying down our own comfort and even reputation to pursue each other's holiness. In *Love Your Enemies*, American sociologist Arthur C. Brooks summarizes people's common responses when people offend us: "(1) ignore, (2) insult, or (3) destroy" them (in person or online).[8] Brooks offers a fourth option, which echoes Jesus: "Love your enemies and pray for those who persecute you" (Matt. 5:44). Love requires listening, and love means engaging honestly when disagreements arise. In Matthew 18, Jesus explains what to do "if your brother sins against you" (v. 15). If I claim to love my children but never discipline them, I misunderstand love! If Jess loves me, she risks my momentary frustration toward her to correct unwisdom or unholiness in my life. Christians "reprove, rebuke," "teach and correct one another" (2 Tim 4:2; Col. 3:16 NIrV). We give and receive discipline in love, in care for each other's holiness. But our standard and posture matter.

101 WAYS TO MOVE FROM FAÇADE TO FAMILY

49 Invite a spiritual sibling over for a meal, outside of church-scheduled events. Invite everyone in your close spiritual family over, outside of church-scheduled events!

50 Make meals collaborative—everyone contributes to potlucks or theme nights, whether little or much.

51 Create an "open table": make extra helpings at meals, so people can drop in without notice.

52 Be okay with PB&J: sharing a meal doesn't need to be fancy; inviting people into your real life can involve the simplest of sandwiches or microwave meals (or even—gasp—leftovers)!

"Church discipline" used to conjure in my mind an overdramatic image of a 1950s agent arriving on someone's doorstep in a trench coat and fedora, serving notice to a surprised sinner. That's not the biblical imagery at all! Some churches ignore discipline altogether, misinterpreting Jesus' words, "Judge not, that you be not judged" (Matt. 7:1). Jesus did not disallow us from pointing out sin or folly in others' lives. He tells us to do exactly that, but to humbly acknowledge our own sin first. "*First* take the log out of your own eye, and *then* you will see clearly to take the speck out of your brother's eye" (v. 5). The Bible specifically charges us to correct others, but based on God's objective standards rather than our personal preferences or convictions. Thus, Paul says our "teaching, . . . reproof, . . . correction, and . . . training in righteousness" is to be based on "Scripture [which] is breathed out by God," and "not to quarrel over [personal] opinions" (2 Tim. 3:16; Rom. 14:1).

In some churches, spiritual discipline feels more like criminal proceedings than a pursuit of discipleship and restoration. We must remember, "discipline" has the same root as "discipleship." Discipline's first step reads, "If your brother sins against you, go and tell him his fault" (Matt. 18:15). If we dwell in honest relationships, bringing sin or hurt to light can happen in informal ways. Just as I correct my kids in stores or car rides, so can we bring up sin with spiritual siblings in simple, everyday conversations. And "if he listens to you, you have gained your brother" (v. 15). Hard but informal conversations bring restoration and holiness. If a one-on-one conversation doesn't work, adding close mutual siblings to the conversation is a picture of communal discipleship. They help the accuser and accused understand each other, protecting and serving both parties. And so the process goes—all in a posture of love, seeking the mutual good, laying down our reputations and fear of others, and being bold, humble, and willing to discipline one another is sacrificial service.

"WELL DONE"

Jesus told His followers a parable of a "master" (representing God) who gives His servants various amounts of "talents." We often think "gifting" or "skill" when we hear "talent," and the principle rings true—but at Jesus' time, a talent was instead a significant amount of money. These servants were to steward their master's possessions well on his behalf. The principle is still true beyond finance: *all* God gives us in our brief lives—time, finances, resources, Bible knowledge, and even relationships—is valuable, and truly belongs to Him. Our stuff has little eternal value, so we use it for God's purposes while we can.

One servant in Jesus' story is fearful and squanders his talent and is rebuked by the master. The rest use their talents well, producing fruit for the master, and receiving rewards for faithfully stewarding their master's resources. As Jesus' followers in a close spiritual family, our joyful duty is using all we have for the common good. As we do, Jesus' parable tells us the commendation we will one day receive from our true Master: "Well done, good and faithful servant. . . . Enter into the joy of your master" (Matt. 25:21).

GOOD SHEPHERDS

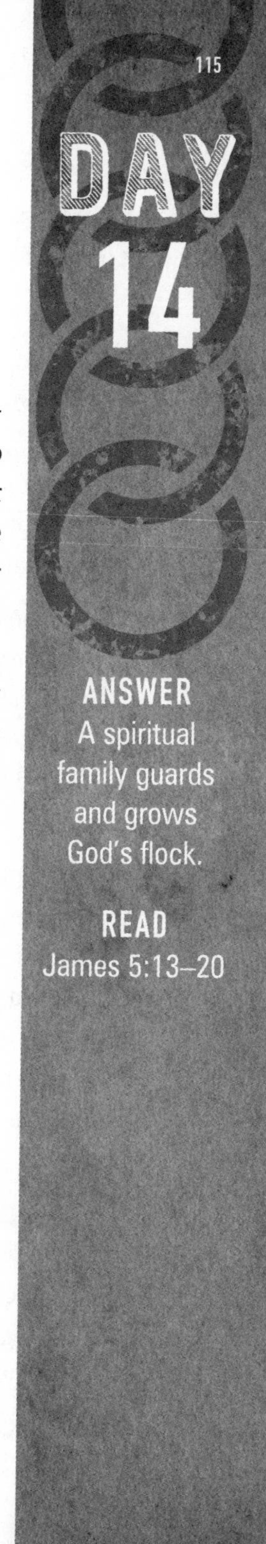

I GREW UP ON A FARM.

It was not large—especially by Texas's standards—but our fourteen acres produced hay, so my preteen job was driving a tractor while older boys tossed and stacked square bales on the trailer behind me. We had horses, barn cats for the mice and snakes, and dogs. And every year, we purchased a few young goats and sheep. While I am far removed from ancient Israel, my view of "shepherding" was shaped by actually raising lambs. Still today as I read "the Lord is my shepherd," and that Jesus is both the "Chief Shepherd" and sacrificial "Lamb of God," images from my childhood come to mind. When I read Jesus' charges to "feed my sheep," care for God's flock, and separate sheep from goats, I recall experiences of doing exactly those things.[9]

Reflecting God's heart toward His people, we cared for, sheltered, and protected our sheep. We nourished, exercised, and strengthened them. (Unlike God's heart, we did all this so our sheep and goats brought the highest price at the annual livestock show, after which my college fund grew while the animals . . . well . . . reflected Jesus' own sacrificial death for my benefit? . . . Every metaphor breaks down.)

The point is that the Bible's many "sheep" and "shepherd" metaphors help us know how to interact with our spiritual siblings (or to follow today's image, our fellow sheep in God's flock). And while this may surprise us, many biblical references invite *every* Christian to shepherd others—not just paid professional "pastors."

"PASTORS" VS. "PASTORING"

Contrary to popular belief, "pastor" is not a title or office God gives church leaders in the Bible. On Day 12 we learned that in Ephesians 4:11–12, "shepherds" are among the giftings God gave to equip His church for holistic, mutual maturity. The Greek word for "shepherd" in Ephesians 4 is ποιμένας, and five aspects of the term help us know what our spiritual families do.

- First, ποιμήν (the root word of the term "shepherd" in Eph. 4) is the same word used for "pastor"—the English terms "pastor" and "shepherd" are literally one word in ancient Greek, and are used interchangeably in the Bible.[10] To "pastor" is to "shepherd" and vice versa, hard stop; there cannot be any difference between these terms in our minds.
- Second, Ephesians 4:11 is the only time the New Testament applies the word to humans on a spiritual level. The term typically references actual shepherds (like those who the angels announced Jesus' birth to in Luke 2), and Jesus uses it as a metaphor in His parables and trainings (e.g., John 10). In the rest of the New Testament, when the term is a noun or title, it always applies to Jesus alone.
- Third, outside the single human occurence of "pastor" or "shepherd" as a noun, both English words in the New Testament are always verbs: "ποιμαίνω (shepherding, pastoring) . . . focuses on 'tending' ('shepherding'), which includes guarding, guiding, and folding the flock and is only provided (ultimately) by Jesus Christ—the Shepherd, who calls undershepherds (*such as [but not limited to]* elder-overseers) to guard and guide His people by His direction (1 Peter 5:1–5)."[11]

- ➜ Fourth, nowhere in Ephesians 4 does God limit verse 11's giftings to church leadership: they are instead given to many members of God's family. *We all participate in building one another up.* If we use the title "pastor" for some church leaders, should our leader teams not necessarily include individuals with the verse's other four titles?

- ➜ Fifth and finally, the Bible *does* give clear titles for church leaders, but those are distinct from the "pastor" or "shepherd." God calls some leaders "elder" or "overseer" (πρεσβύτερος and ἐπίσκοπος, respectively), and others "deacon" or "servant" (both from the term διάκονος).

We could go into detail on each element, but I hope you enjoyed today's Greek class!

SHEEPDOGS AND FELLOW SHEEP

Why does this word study matter? Because we cannot limit the "pastoring" or "shepherding" of God's people to a few paid or volunteer leaders. Leading, protecting, feeding, and nourishing are aspects of pastoring, and it's something God calls all of His people to!

Elders (the title) must participate in the work of pastoring (the verb) God's flock. But elders are "under-shepherds" at best, helping God's flock follow our one "Chief Shepherd," Jesus.[12] American professor Harold Senkbeil takes the image further, viewing church leaders not even as under-shepherds, but sheepdogs: "The sheepdog is iconic of a faithful [leader's] work: one ear tuned to the voice of the Great Shepherd, the other tuned attentively to the sheep."[13]

And while leaders must participate in shepherding the flock, every Christian has a role in this work! "Shepherding" is work God designed His people to do together. We are called and gifted to "pastor" each other in various ways. My experience with actual sheep affirms that herd mentality is real: what one sheep does others do. I remember pouring grain into a trough in our lean-to, closed off to the weather on three sides but clearly open on the fourth. A sheep heard the sound and sprinted toward it, while others mindlessly followed. The first sheep reached the lean-to at full speed, missed the open side and ran—*smack*—into one of the three walls. The others followed its lead—*smack, smack, smack, smack* . . . then did so *again* as the first sheep missed the opening a second time and head-butted the wall *again*!

This isn't a flattering image, but it's one I remember of a literal flock representing a spiritual one: most shepherding of God's people doesn't require leaders' involvement; much of it happens as God's people dwell in familial relationship, taking responsibility for and using their giftings for others. If everyone waits for someone else to lead the charge, it will never happen. But if someone—anyone—goes first, others will follow. As spiritual siblings, we do the good work of ministry and mission together, of building each other up, and of speaking truth in love together.

EXAMPLES AMONG ONE FLOCK

"Mutual shepherding" has many elements, but considering today's passage from James, I will share three examples of how God's people can shepherd each other well.

1. *"Confess Your Sins"*

No one likes to admit weakness. Most of us hate confessing sin, before God or other people! But when we let others into our need and disobedience, we stop fighting alone and others can help us. Todd was honest with some men in my group recently about his tendency to pursue a second drink whenever he drank alcohol. He had recognized this pattern for a while, but when he started hiding his follow-up drink, he wanted to let others in. Todd was nowhere close to a drunk or alcoholic. He simply noticed something that raised a yellow flag—and instead of hiding, he brought trusted men into his life.

We asked Todd questions and gave insights; some spoke of similar desires. I mentioned respective days I'd thought, *That was a good day; I should celebrate with a drink*, and then, *Man today was rough; a drink sounds nice*. Again, no overt drunkenness existed, but sinful desire and motive came to light around the circle. We prayed for each other, a few of us committed to a monthlong alcohol fast to test our desires and turn our minds toward Jesus, and we followed up with each other—all because Todd was vulnerable and obedient to God's command to confess sin to one another, and because others entered into the honesty, returned it, and shared each other's burdens. The following months, God worked in Todd and the rest of us, and we all grew more mature in our view and use of alcohol.

2. *"Pray for One Another"*

James 5:14 refers to elders praying in the face of suffering and sickness—but also says we can all pray for others. Elijah was a simple man, James says, "with a nature like ours," but God heard his "fervent" prayer (v. 17). "The prayer of [*any*] righteous person has great power as it is working" (v. 16). The men mentioned above prayed with Todd and one another, and God answered our prayers.

On a separate occasion, after three years of increasing, unending, undiagnosed sickness and a sense of "spiritual darkness" in the home they had lived in for over eight years, Ashley and Kurtis obeyed this passage from James 5 and invited friends—two elders along with a man and woman from their own City Group—to pray over the rooms of their house and anoint them with oil. You don't know me, but while I'm not a "demon-under-every-rock" guy, I believe in spiritual warfare and demonic oppression because the Bible tells me both are real. I join many orthodox believers in thinking that demons can be spiritually assigned to specific places. So we went room by room through Kurtis and Ashley's house, anointing door posts with oil, dedicating each room to the Lord, praying for deliverance from sickness and oppression, and asking God to remove darkness and demonic influence from each room. Marvin was with us. He is not an elder, but man does Marvin pray! He led us well, and we prayed over the whole house in a couple hours.

Praise God, in the two weeks that followed our prayers, they finally got answers and effective treatment for the sickness. Ashley's rashes, peeling skin, and hives were visibly gone, and her severe itching and immune system problems were reduced significantly and continued to improve as time went on. And the darkness in the air of the home had lifted.

3. *"Bring . . . Back a Sinner"*

A final image of a sheep and shepherd in this passage is bringing a sinner back from their wandering. "If a man has a hundred sheep, and one of them has gone astray," Jesus similarly taught, "does he not leave the ninety-nine on the mountains and go in search of the one that went astray? And if he finds it, truly, I say to you, he rejoices over it more than over the ninety-nine that never went astray" (Matt. 18:12–13). Every time a Christian chases someone who slipped away, we reflect the prodigal son's father. We pursue wayward friends, boldly and compassionately speak God's truth, and try to bring straying sheep back, from both overt sins like adultery, addiction, and anger, and subtle ones like pride, greed, and love of comfort. Whether people come back or not, our care, prayer, and

101 WAYS TO MOVE FROM FAÇADE TO FAMILY

53 Pray together—often: praise God as the source of things we celebrate; depend on Him in areas of need.

54 Be publicly prayerful: in conflict resolution, while sharing truth, or when needs arise, prayer displays our trust that God knows and cares more than you.

55 Be privately prayerful: pray for your close spiritual family! Thank God for them daily, celebrating joys and lifting up needs.

56 Bear burdens: don't take "no" for an answer, and don't let anyone wrestle alone—proactively enter each other's pain.

pursuit is an example of obedient shepherding that can exist among all God's sheep, not just from sheepdog leaders.

EVERYDAY SHEPHERDING

References to shepherding each other fill the New Testament: "Let the word of Christ dwell in you richly," Paul exhorts everyday Christians, "teaching and admonishing one another in all wisdom" (Col. 3:16). God charges an entire community to "guard your hearts and your minds in Christ Jesus," to "exhort one another every day, as long as it is called 'today,'" and to "rebuke those who contradict . . . instruction in sound doctrine."[14]

Two great men married my two sisters. But if I had known something terrible about either that a sister did not know before they got married, it would have been unloving to keep it from her and let the relationship proceed. Mutual shepherding is not just affirming fellow sheep; we do hard things for each other's good. "Beware of false prophets, who come to you in sheep's clothing but inwardly are ravenous wolves," Jesus warned.[15] No wolves lived on my childhood farm, but coyotes and snakes did. Our commitment to the flock must involve caring for each other, protecting each other, and guarding each other from falsehood and spiritual danger. Even if we occasionally hurt fellow sheep, "faithful are the wounds of a friend."[16]

Do you see yourself as a sheep, called to care for other sheep? Tangible examples of shepherding occur throughout the Bible, and we can grow in this ability throughout our lives. But shepherding other sheep—pastoring our spiritual siblings—is what a spiritual family does as we take mutual responsibility seriously and care for each other as much as we care for ourselves.

WEEK THREE IN ACTION

The last day of each week you will read how churches across the world live as a family and will discuss this week's content with others. As you discuss the questions, be honest with yourself and others, and let them speak truth in love as you put this book into practice together.

LIVING AS FAMILY: COMUNIDAD MOSAICO, LEÓN, MEXICO

Family is important to Mexicans. We don't distinguish between "nuclear" or "extended." *Familia* is simply *familia*. From cradle to the grave, our lives revolve around family rhythms and celebrations. In our culture, when a baby is baptized, the entire family goes to the church. The family prepares a large meal and invites friends, neighbors, and the priest. Young and old celebrate and take part in the party. Most significant life events call for a family celebration, from first communions to the buying of a new home. Even traditional food is family-centered. For example, making tamales during Christmas involves the entire family. Mom makes the savory and sweet fillings, and the other adults assemble them while the children play. We view identity through the lens of family. But if celebrations are fruits, then the Catholic Church is the tree. When a person becomes a Protestant Christian, the entire family feels it. It is as if the family loses a part. The person becomes an exile from his or her family and its celebrations.

Most of Soma Mosaico's, our church's, activities happen at homes around a meal. For example, our young men's group meets at homes, around tables. The men prepare a quick meal before studying theology. This gives us time to check in and see how everyone is doing. We hear about work and school. There's time to joke around. For these young men, it has a familiar feeling. It feels like when cousins hang out.

Our Missional Communities also meet for a meal at least weekly. As people arrive, they say hi to every person: it's important that everyone feels seen as part of the group. Like *familia*, we chat and laugh. The older women worry about people not wearing jackets when it's cold, or people not eating enough. Kids run around. It feels like an ordinary meal with gospel intentionality. We hear how Jesus is transforming lives or areas where we each struggle. The whole family listens, then responds. That's what families do. Our leaders

101 WAYS TO MOVE FROM FAÇADE TO FAMILY

57 Practice declaring the gospel (and as you speak truth into each other's stories and situations, your ability and confidence grows toward speaking God's truth with non believers).

58 Be honest about imperfections: don't hide faults, mistakes, sins, and conflict. Talk about your humanness, and the fruit God produces as He matures you.

59 Be humble: work against sins of entitlement, selfishness, reputation, and pride, and consider others more highly than yourself.

60 Be honoring: a friend once said, "The Bible only commends competition once: 'outdo one another in showing honor' (Rom. 12:10)." Honor others regularly and well!

focus on teaching the church to speak the gospel as a second language by modeling it around a meal. Hours pass and people don't want to leave. It's more than a meal; it's the gospel restoring something each person has culturally lost. Yes, we're exiles, but we're not alone. We get to travel this life as a family.

Atanasio Segovia

"WHAT" QUESTIONS TO DISCUSS

- ☐ **GENERAL:** What impacted you most this week? What was new, convicting, difficult, or confusing? What biblical truths do you need others to remind you of, in love?
- ☐ **GENERAL:** What are some ways you and other Christians have historically lived as family together? In what ways is this week's content different from your past experience?
- ☐ **DAY 11:** Why do you think Christians can have a hard time practicing love, encouragement, unity, sympathy, tenderheartedness, humility, and blessing?
- ☐ **DAY 11:** Of 1 Peter's "one another" commands, which do you feel most fruitful in practicing? Which do you need growth in? How will you pursue growth this week?
- ☐ **DAY 12:** What do you base your spiritual growth on, other than "speaking truth in love"? How does God use Christians "speaking truth in love" together to mature His body?
- ☐ **DAY 12:** What are areas you need to grow up spiritually? Who in your close spiritual family is gifted in those areas—how do they work with you for your growth?
- ☐ **DAY 13:** What resources do you have that could serve, bless, and care for others? What would you have to overcome to use them like that?

☐ **DAY 13:** What might God be calling you to sacrifice, or how might He call you into discomfort for His glory and others' good? How can others help you take those steps with faith, humility, and boldness?

☐ **DAY 14:** What does it mean that that every Christian can be involved in shepherding and care for each other? How does that compare or contrast to your church experience?

☐ **DAY 14:** What ways can your close spiritual family commit to care for and shepherd each other? (Examples: James 5:16–20; Col. 3:16; Phil. 4:7; Heb. 3:13)

☐ **GENERAL:** Considering Day 11's reference to learning stories, how can your close spiritual family make time to share and listen to each other's stories as a stronger foundation for speaking truth in love? (See Appendix A for resources.)

☐ **GENERAL:** Look over this week's "101 Ways." What else could you do, per your own gifting, spiritual family, and mission field, to live as God's family? Post ideas with the hashtag, #genuine community.

WEEK FOUR

WHEN AND WHERE DOES A SPIRITUAL FAMILY INTERACT?

"IT'S TIME FOR CHURCH."

As a boy, my dad attended mass every Sunday. Raised Roman Catholic, he recalls the level to which this was a priority to his own father (my grandfather). If young Dennis felt sick one Sunday morning, his dad would ask if Dennis needed to throw up. If Dennis responded no, his dad would declare him well enough for mass. If Dennis responded yes, his dad would tell him to get on with it and that he would feel better when done so he could get in the car. At least that's how my dad tells it—likely only half joking. This is an extreme picture of a common theme in many Christian veins: we highly prioritize gathering together on Sundays—at times to the exclusion of any other gatherings of God's people.

During the COVID pandemic, my church's leaders—like all others—analyzed various aspects of discipleship across our church family. We debated holding in-person Sunday gatherings vs. remaining online. Karl, an elder, mentioned a comment he'd heard from a church member, saying he had grown "spiritually dry" during the pandemic, specifically because he "had not been able to hear any sermons." Karl got to serve, press, and encourage this member, but the comment points to an issue that is true in many churches, whether Catholic or Protestant. When I relayed the story to my wife, Jess, she became upset: "If his relationship with God is that reliant on a preacher, it's no different than how I grew up, where a priest was the only way we could hear from God."

To be clear, I am pro-preaching and pro-Sunday gathering. So is Jess. In over twenty years in church leadership, I've preached hundreds of sermons. I believe God produced fruit in His people through those gatherings and sermons. (At least some of them!) But sermons are insufficient to produce *all* the fruit in people. Regular peer-to-peer discipleship, in the context of a small group of committed, diverse sisters and brothers in Christ, is where most discipleship takes place. That's what we see in the Bible, and that's what we've seen so far in this book. This week we build on that theme, asking questions like: "What would happen if Christians devoted themselves to each other in everyday life as much as they do to Sunday attendance?" "What if we committed to using our gifts and speaking truth in love in many times and places throughout the week, as much as to singing songs and consuming a sermon for sixty to ninety minutes on Sunday?"

The Church is God's body and family; it is not an event or building. While God warns against "neglecting to meet together" (Heb. 10:25), only recently has that verse been used to describe large Sunday gatherings. If discipleship happens among smaller groups of spiritual siblings, and if we grow in obedience to many of God's commands through regular interactions with others, we must enter each other's lives the six-days-and-twenty-two-and-a-half-hours between Sunday gatherings. So Week Four answers the dual question, "When and Where Does a Spiritual Family Interact?" We'll see that—contrary to our church member's erroneous thinking above—God can produce fruit nearly any place and time His children pursue intentional discipleship and relationship together.

DAY 16

ANSWER
We are a devoted family "day by day."

READ
Acts 2:42–47

"DAY BY DAY"

WHAT ARE YOU "DEVOTED" TO?

You're likely devoted to your family or relationship, or to your job or studies. You may be devoted to an ideal or cause, or perhaps a political figure, musician, or sports team. Or maybe you merely *claim* devotion to these or other things. It's easy to claim commitment to a person, place, thing, or idea until someone presses hard or digs deep. True devotion is marked by willingness to put time, money, and effort into something. What we prioritize—and sacrifice for—are what we're actually devoted to.

Fans who follow their favorite band from city to city sacrifice money for gas, lodging, and tickets; they sacrifice time with friends, family, and work—but the benefit outweighs the cost; they're devoted to the band. Many people save for plane tickets and lodging and plan annual time off; we're devoted to summer holidays. We cannot put our phones away on weekends; we're devoted to work (ouch). And so forth. Devotion means prioritization; devotion requires sacrifice, good or bad.

In Acts 2, Jesus' early followers were devoted. This devotion came at great cost. Early Christians were disowned by families for abdicating the faith of their heritage. They were arrested and killed by Jewish and Roman leaders. As we'll see today, they sacrificed time and treasure, and put aside other relationships and priorities. They gave up a lot—but the benefit outweighed the cost; they were devoted to God and each other.

This week we're asking, "When and where does a spiritual family interact?" Acts 2 answers both sides of the question: "Day by day [history's first Christians attended] the temple together and [broke] bread in their homes" (Acts 2:46). *Great*, we might think, *if I go to church on Sunday and see my Christian community one other day, I've made it*. Unfortunately, like many verses used to prove any stance or belief, there's more to this we need to uncover. Motives matter more than actions: so yes, early Christians interacted "when" they saw each other day by day. Yes, homes and public spaces were "where" they gathered. But true, deep devotion was the motive for God's people to interact "day by day." Spiritual families are designed to be in each other's lives in simple ways, often. Acts 2:42–47 shows us how this "day by day" life can look.

DEVOTION TO GOD'S WORD

A spiritual family is first devoted to God's Word. Acts 2 and other verses show God's first-century people together far more than once a week and regularly in God's Word. Today, even the best preachers lack the spiritual authority of Jesus' original apostles. While preaching can be helpful for spiritual formation, and while we should view it is a sacred task for God's glory, preachers are at best imperfect commenters on God's perfect Word! So day by day devotion to "the apostles' teaching" today must surpass weekly sermons and discussing that sermon later with others, using planned questions whose answers stem from Pastor So-and-So's imperfect commentary more than the perfect biblical text.

Followers of Jesus replicate the early church's devotion to the authoritative teaching of Jesus' apostles when they learn directly from the inspired words that some of those apostles wrote! The Protestant Reformation rallied every Christian to approach God directly and read the Bible on their own. But many Christians today are content reverting to seeing preachers as functional mediators:

a preacher can access God, and knowledge or godliness is mediated through his preaching. No! God calls *all His people* to "let the word of Christ dwell in you richly, teaching and admonishing one another in all wisdom" (Col. 3:16); and part of the Holy Spirit's ministry is teaching us God's will—whether directly, from God's Word, or through each other (Ps. 143:10).

I was involved with a Canadian ministry for a time. One of the most shaping elements of that season was the unity and commonality that existed across the organization's leaders simply by committing to the same Bible reading plan each year. Every day, people across Canada (and a few of us 'Muricans too) learned directly from the same chapters as our colleagues and others. The number of times a given morning's reading would enter a seemingly unrelated staff conversation or coaching call later that day was astounding. Similarly, everyone involved in WeAreChurch, a network of churches in California, read through the Bible together annually, following the same plan. Their leaders talk about the unity and camaraderie that's built when one member sees another at a cafe, and in the course of the conversation, one says, "That reminds me of what God said this morning in Isaiah" or "What did you think about Romans 12 today?" It's beautiful when everyday Christians grow in depth and obedience, together. This happens as we read and discuss God's Word together in everyday ways.

GOD'S PEOPLE

The rest of Acts 2:42 describes how a shared devotion to God's Word overflowed into devotion to others: "They devoted themselves to . . . the fellowship, to the breaking of bread and the prayers." I explained the word "fellowship" in this book's introduction: deeper and more regular than a church gathering or small group meeting, "fellowship" does not describe small talk at a Sunday coffee cart, or name a "hall" in a church building where receptions happen, or the "down time" before a group meeting "gets going." *Koinónia* is intimate, ongoing participation and deep communion for mutual benefit. It's the co-ownership and the deep responsibility members of the early church felt for each other's growth, health, and discipleship.

This everyday interaction and known-ness overflowed into sharing meals, care, and prayers together. "Breaking bread" was not likely a planned weekly event, and "prayers" were not relegated to the final five minutes of a group meeting. Rather, prayers were cries of desperation, begging God to save lives, free jailed friends, and to both protect and use Christians—even in their suffering—to share the gospel and spread God's kingdom across the land. Prayer was urgent and reliant; it acknowledged God's authority and enacted His power and strength.

Care similarly went beyond a Meal Train sign up or a church's benevolence fund. Early Christians were truly devoted to meet every need and personally sacrificed for others. "All who believed were together and had all things in common. And they were selling their possessions and belongings and distributing the proceeds to all, as any had need" (vv. 44–45). This picture is so foreign to Christians shaped by individualism and consumerism that I must reiterate: it was *literal*, not figurative. This is not overinflated or idealized. Actual people actually used what God had actually given them, to actually meet others' actual needs—and not even for a tax write-off! They personally (not through an organization), joyfully (without grumbling), sacrificially (not selfishly), holistically (not just spiritually) met needs "with glad and generous hearts" (not from obligation or stinginess). Could churches today display God's care for us by devoting ourselves to this kind of care for others?

Finally, "breaking bread" was a family affair in the first century: culturally everyone contributed any food they had, and if someone had nothing, they simply received. The first Christians ate together often. On numerous occasions, people from my church family have been at my house—kids playing, adults talking—and rather than send them home, we simply decide to eat together. Sometimes it's leftovers, other times pasta or whatever we find in the fridge. If one adult is on his or her way over, they grab their own leftovers or occasionally pick up fajitas or Thai food (mmmm). In shared life, meals together aren't fancy; they can just happen!

Doxa Church in Bellevue, WA, launches new groups with an eight-week "Pilot Group." To help people understand the level of devotion in groups, "the church" provides a meal the first week; the other seven, each group brings portions of a shared meal. Among other training elements, this requires sacrifice and buy-in: a Doxa value reads, "We are contributors, not consumers."[1] Jeff Vanderstelt, one of Doxa's leaders, teaches regularly how shared meals can lead to *the meal*: historically, Christian observances of communion or The Lord's Supper happened during an actual meal around a table, not via a somber breadcrumb and juice shot at a Sunday gathering. Through day by day "fellowship," deep prayer, and shared meals, God's people beautifully devote themselves to each other.

WHOLE-LIFE WORSHIP AND GOD'S MISSION

We misinterpret Acts 2 if we think "attending the temple" (v. 46) was a first-century equivalent to "going to church." First, the

101 WAYS TO MOVE FROM FAÇADE TO FAMILY

61 When a spiritual sibling is sick, run errands, watch kids, provide food, and find ways to help.

62 When you're sick, humble yourself by asking others for their help!

63 When a new baby arrives, take meals, run errands, and help with chores or childcare for older kids—involve others to collaborate and serve them well!

64 Throw wedding or baby showers to surround and provide for the grown family's new season.

Jerusalem temple continued as the site of Jewish—not Christian—worship until its destruction in AD 70. Christians worshiping at the temple would be more like attending a synagogue or mosque today than attending a Sunday morning church service. Second, temple worship did not involve elements of today's "church services." Worship revolved around the animal sacrifices from Leviticus 1–6. Jews brought an animal to offer, and a priest would sacrifice it for their sin. New Christians believed Jesus' death covered their sins once and for all, and there was no need for a priest to mediate between God and man; Jesus alone was that Priest. So when early Christians went to the temple, they publicly demonstrated and declared the gospel to friends, family, and even the people who persecuted and rejected them. Christians devoted themselves to worship and mission.

"Awe came upon every soul, and many wonders and signs were being done through the apostles" (v. 43); "attending the temple together and breaking bread in their homes, they [were] . . . praising God and having favor with all the people" (vv. 46–47). Most sermons in the New Testament happened publicly, in the midst of not-yet believers.[2] Many of the apostles' signs and wonders—which fulfilled Jesus' promise, "whoever believes in me will also do the works that I do" (John 14:12)—occurred in view of both people who believed and people who didn't. Many acts, songs, and words of praise in the New Testament similarly occurred in public spaces. My friend and church leader Bob Roberts Jr. charges Christians to live out our faith "in the public square," in part because that's how the early church lived. They were devoted to worship, not through Jewish temple rituals they left behind, but through whole-life devotion to God and each other and through sacrificial love, even for their enemies. They were devoted to mission, not as an occasional activity for a certain time, but as they demonstrated and declared the gospel publicly and winsomely, in everyday life. And God worked through their devotion: "The Lord added to their number day by day those who were being saved" (v. 47).

RECLAIMING DEVOTION

We need to consider our own devotion—to God, each other, worship, and mission. The first-century church went "all in" on a few commitments, with a few people, and sacrificed everything for them. Worship, mission, serving others, prayer, and learning from God happened in everyday life, in everyday ways. They weren't reliant on a Sunday service, a certain preacher, or a benevolence fund—they did not even have printed Bibles for centuries! But through whole-life devotion to God, each other, worship, and mission, the Church grew and the gospel spread at a rate unseen since. Could it be that in all the centralization, strategies, and loose interaction with dozens or hundreds of people that we miss the key to mutual growth in Christ? When and where does a spiritual family interact? In its best and purest form, it's deeply devoting ourselves to God, each other, worship, and mission—and doing so "day by day."

UNFILTERED LIVES

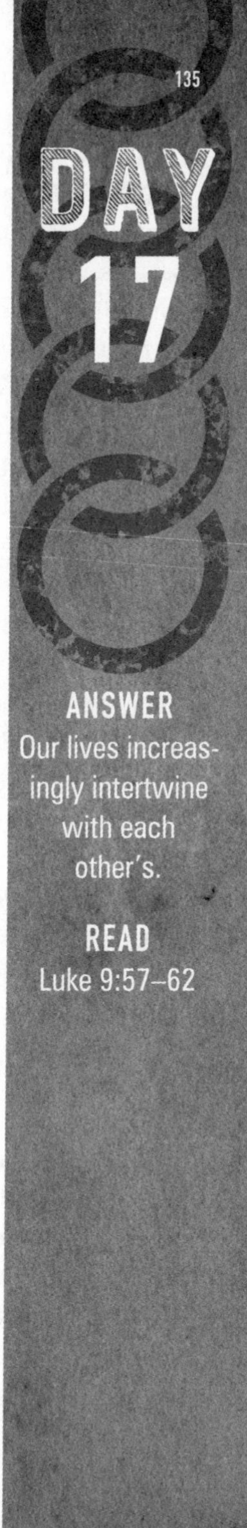

LIFE ONLINE IS DANGEROUS.

The internet can be helpful: we interact with friends and family in different cities; we get updates and insights from across the globe in a millisecond; and from dating to affinity groups to online games, we connect with people we would otherwise not know. But the internet's dangers are innumerable. I will not outline them all, but one digital danger can be a warning for our actual lives: we can present and posture ourselves any way we want online, whether that's our actual reality or not.

We post amazing pictures of a beach's sunset on Instagram, cropping out the garbage dump just out of frame. We tweet a winsome tweet we didn't *exactly* plagiarize but got pretty close. We airbrush and filter away blemishes. We edit our "stories" to perfection. We find the perfectly humble words as we re-post someone's affirmation of us. And of course, we show off our #blessed lives. In this, we delight our virtual "friends" (who we sometimes know in real life) and "followers" (who would seldom follow us in real life), who reward our digital prowess in the currency of "reactions." They seem like cheap rewards for all the time we spend on perfect posts. But similarly, those posts are cheap replacements for our actual lives.

DIGITAL REALITY IN ACTUAL LIFE

I get it. I'm not great or consistent on social media, but I have to guard against finding worth in the number or type of "reactions" a post gets. The digital reality is a trap—but I don't believe the concept is limited to the internet. Every human tends to airbrush, edit, crop, and filter our actual lives too, presenting the version of ourselves we want others to see, know, and love. And for Christians, "putting on our Sunday best" means we often hide our true selves, deepest hurts, and greatest needs even when we are with our church families.

Have you ever had a family fight on the way to a church gathering—perhaps declaring a ceasefire and donning plastic smiles in the foyer, then halfway listened to a sermon while building the perfect case against your spouse, and resumed hostilities as the van door closed? Or have you ever yearned to share a sin struggle with someone, only to chicken out for fear they'd judge you or you'd feel ashamed? Or have you ever half-confessed a sin, looking contrite enough to convince others while never actually desiring to put it to death?

Many Christian relationships might be described as "seldom and shallow" rather than "often and deep." That kind of relationship hinders the "devoted" life we saw yesterday. Façades keep us from growing together and from reaching the depth of relationship God calls us to. A spiritual family grows together as our lives increasingly intertwine with each other's. This means others need to see our real lives—however messy they are.

GOING DEEP

SCUBA training is required before people suit up and plunge into the ocean's depths. Failure to prepare is dangerous. In fact, SCUBA is a risky endeavor—but if people prepare well, the beauty and adventure are worth the risk. Similarly, there is both risk and beauty in pursuing the depth of relationships God has for His people. To intertwine our life with others to the degree we've seen, we must consider (and maybe reorient) our time and relationships, our words, and our location.

Prioritizing Time and Relationships

Time, more and more voices tell us, is the most valuable resource we have, so we must use it well.[3] Jesus had three short years of public ministry on earth and devoted much of it to a small band of close followers—never more than 120, mostly 12, and often only Peter, James, and John. Jesus occasionally taught large crowds, debated religious rulers, and performed healings and exorcisms, but most of His life was walking, talking, teaching, and training His close followers. Jesus chose to forgo crowds to instead focus on those who counted the cost of obedience and went "all in" with Him. He encouraged His disciples to shake the dust off their feet if people wouldn't receive them. He allowed the rich young ruler to walk away, unwilling to give up everything for Jesus. And Jesus left the crowds to pray or to spend time with His closest followers. Jesus consistently went deep with few, instead of shallow with many.

We already saw that people can generally have five to fifteen meaningful relationships. But are we willing to follow Jesus' example, accept our relational limitations, and open our lives often to a few people to know well? Will we even prioritize those relationships at the expense of others? Many people could help shape us spiritually in some way through occasional interactions. We may engage for a season with a specific mentor, counselor, or person gifted in an area we're weak. And God might direct us toward new, additional, or different relationships as we seek Him. But every conversation, meal, and relationship takes time. Objectively, we spend eternity with every other believer we know—so the most valuable way to prioritize our time on earth is to give and receive regularly with the few people who form your (variously gifted, multi-perspective, multiethnic, cross-generational) spiritual family of God.

Prioritizing Our Words

Once we've chosen to devote ourselves to consistent relationships, we truly start going deep . . . and this takes time. My church's multiple groups show that it often takes a year or more to let down guards and reach a level of trust and openness with others. Your close spiritual family can book a weekend away together, with a mix of intentional conversation and fun. You can get to know each other by sharing your stories with Jesus as the hero (see Appendix A). You can ask "What if . . ." questions, play party games, and walk-through exercises that describe hopes, identities, and fears.

The key to this is a willingness to both speak and listen. When we replace pride, reputation, and people-pleasing tendencies with a willingness to share openly, reflect honesty, speak with grace, and display love (even in disagreement), we start building trust. When we speak well—about God in a way that glorifies Him, about ourselves with humility, and about others in a way that builds up—relationship deepens, growth happens, and God is glorified. Even more important than just speaking well, we must listen well. Proverbs tells us, "The purpose in a man's heart is like deep water, but a man of understanding will draw it out" (Prov. 20:5). Our willingness to lay aside our agendas, withhold our comments, and patiently listen displays the "one anothers" discussed earlier. Asking good follow-up questions, listening for motives, fears, idols, and values in peoples' stories and comments, helps us know them better and see how the gospel is—and isn't—good news. Christians are known for our desire to share our opinions with others but listening opens the door to serve others well.

Prioritizing Our Location

A third priority to consider as we regularly go deep with a few people is our willingness to have people into our homes, and our willingness to go into theirs. Neutral ground is "safe": If I only see other Christians in the building my church gathers or at a restaurant, park, or coffee shop, I can maintain a level of comfort and distance; I don't have to clean or worry about being served a dish I don't like, and I can maintain my privacy. If I only enter someone's house or have people into mine a set night of the week, everything can be in its place, the kids and kitchen can be clean, and the space is warm and inviting.

We've already said biblical hospitality is good—God wants strangers to feel welcomed. And there are surely times to meet elsewhere. But if we only meet in neutral spaces at scheduled times, we can maintain edited, airbrushed lives. In unexpected pop-ins, people get to know my home and how those in it truly live. In my reaction to them seeing the mess, they see my values and fears. At my kitchen table, deep conversations go late into the night, as no church janitor or barkeep asks us to leave. In my living room, games are played (and competitive idols revealed), reconciliation has been sought, prayers prayed, marriages prepared for, and so forth.

THE MAN BEHIND THE CURTAIN

There's a level of discomfort in prioritizing some relationships over others; in learning to speak and listen well; and in letting people into the privacy of our lives. But without a willingness to engage some risk, we can stay on the surface, hide behind whatever image we want to portray, and remain comfortably unknown. We die to ourselves when we follow Jesus into giving ourselves for others. We

101 WAYS TO MOVE FROM FAÇADE TO FAMILY

65 Move to the same street: Half of my close spiritual family lives within walking distance. It makes everyday discipleship, care, and relationship easier!

66 Stay on that street: If a work promotion requires a move, would you turn it down for the sake of God's family?

67 Cram in: If your family grows but you can stay put—even if your kids share a room or you live in cramped quarters—would you stay for others' sake?

68 Share space: Whether multiple houses on one plot, or multiple couples under one roof, invite some spiritual siblings to live with you and your actual family.

find truer, fuller life in Christ and with His people as we count the cost and declare obedience and love for God and others better than our own comfort and convenience.

In today's passage, Jesus tells us God's kingdom is better than homes, close family duties, or friends and loved ones: "No one who puts his hand to the plow and looks back is fit for the kingdom of God" (Luke 9:62). Jesus calls us to costly lives—which are full and rich in this life, and whose suffering and sacrifice fades in comparison to the glory coming in the next (Rom. 8:18). Not everyone suits up and takes the plunge. (The rich young ruler rejected Jesus to His face!) But to devote ourselves to five to fifteen people, it's OK to prioritize those who are ready and willing. As author and missionary Francis Chan writes, "Either people will be awed by the sacred or they will not. If the sacred is not enough, then it is clear that the Spirit has not done a work in their lives. If the sheep don't hear His voice, let them walk away. Don't call out with your own voice."[4]

The turning point in 1939's *The Wizard of Oz* is Dorothy's dog, Toto, pulling back a curtain and revealing that "Oz the Great and Powerful"—the supposed wizard of the Emerald City—was actually an illusion run by "that man behind the curtain." Oscar Diggs, a circus performer from Nebraska, conjured up the image of a wizard. But it was a façade, as Dorothy and her friends discovered.

Everyone is like Oscar Diggs, but we put ourselves forward as Oz the Great and Powerful. When we go deep with a few people, learn to speak and listen well, and experience each other's true habitats, others get behind our proverbial curtains, and we learn the truth behind theirs. When our lives increasingly intertwine with others, we put down our filters, edits, and cropping tools, and people see who we really are—in our beauty and our messes. But the real version is better than the façade we hide behind—which is, after all, the wonderfully created person God made you to be.

HIGHS, LOWS, AND STATUS QUOS

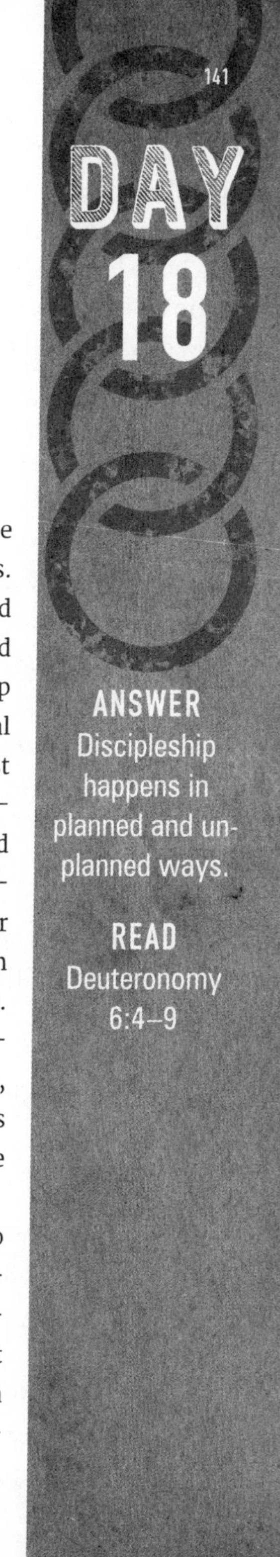

"IT'S 10:53 P.M.," MATT ANNOUNCED SURPRISINGLY.

Jess and I were on Matt and Nicole's porch as the Texas night finally dipped back into double digits. The frozen drinks were long gone; their kids and ours had finished dinner and had self-regulated with surprising success, allowing "grown-up conversation" to meander well past our normal end time. Matt and Nicole are among our closest friends; they have long been comrades in ministry and mission; they are like family. We trust and love each other; we have cared for and encouraged each other; my family has even crashed their family's summer vacation! We have given each other encouragement, advice, and hard words. We've walked through life's "highs"—celebrations, births, milestones—and "lows"—pain, scary moments, and grief. And we've shared lots of moments between highs and lows; they're simply just "life."

This particular evening was full of catch-up and conversation: we shared our plans for summer trips and the upcoming school year, we discussed ethnic injustice and division; we caught up on church life. Nicole shared thoughts on a teaching she was preparing, and they both exhorted me to consider some new responsibilities.

We usually leave around 9:00 p.m., so we were all surprised at Matt's announcement; our typical conversation, on a normal summer night on their porch, was rich and intriguing and lasted two extra hours! We rushed home, our kids washed off bug spray, and we were all in bed as soon as possible. But as we raced away, I realized how much discipleship occurred the previous hours: we experienced many "one another" commands, reminded each other of Scripture and conviction, applied the gospel to things we were each wrestling with, and more—all over dinner and drinks on a back porch one hot summer night.

Jesus experienced high "highs" and low "lows"—many with His disciples at His side. But much of His ministry involved everyday, average conversations with followers and critics. Birds and flowers became object lessons about God's love for us. He engaged discussions and debates, calmly pointing out ways people misunderstood God and His kingdom. All four Gospels—Mark's in particular—display much of Jesus' ministry and teaching as occurring "along the way." He taught as He and His disciples journeyed from one place to another; He ministered on Israel's roads and shores. He met people at their tables and homes, and in marketplaces and fields, as much as in synagogues and the temple. Throughout the New Testament, His followers did the same. We pick up on Jesus' model today, seeing every interaction—formal or informal; planned or not—as an opportunity for discipleship. We can live as a spiritual family anytime, anywhere. Today lists a few examples among many, of how this can look.

EVERYDAY RHYTHMS

We live as a spiritual family when we do things together. Sarah rarely takes her kids to the zoo alone; she brings along another mom with kids. As they wander the pathways and wrestle kids down from animal enclosures, they talk—about life, God, struggles, and joys. One of the most meaningful conversations I've had was with Camp while he gave me a ride to the airport on the way to his nearby office. He meaningfully pointed me toward specific gospel truth in an area

I was doubting God. During a family walk during the COVID-19 lockdown, I got to encourage a neighbor toward trusting God's provision as he wondered aloud about the future of his job.

These are three of a thousand normal rhythms of everyday life. We can walk through much of life with others, whether planned over a text or two (like a zoo trip or morning commute) or walking through the proverbial, unplanned "open doors" God drops into our lives (like a convo during an evening walk) (see Col. 4:3). We can ask questions, discuss our days, and share things we're learning, wondering about, or struggling with anytime we see others. Simply by involving others in rhythms and being intentional with the time, we can share our work, rest, daily tasks. We can go out of our way during "in-between" moments, calling or texting someone we're thinking of, talking and listening well (see yesterday), or doing mostly anything together.

TABLES AND COUCHES

Today's reading shows discipleship in everyday moments: "Talk of [God's character and commands] when you sit in your house, and when you walk by the way, and when you lie down, and when you rise" (Deut. 6:7). More than one person has overcome fear at my family's dinner table and prayed aloud for the first time. Through meals together often, modeling the simplicity of prayer, and inviting others to participate, these people grew in this area of discipleship. Around that same table (specially made by someone in our spiritual family, incidentally, to fit fourteen people), sin has been confessed and love professed, God has been questioned and trusted, and fears, wonders, worries, joys, and pain have been shared as freely as the good drink and comforting food Jess loves to make.

Similarly, Jess and I found solace during difficult times in Todd and Tina's living room. We spent hours on their couch, receiving prayer, comfort, and encouragement from good friends. On that same couch—during that same season, and many times before and since—we have played games, shared laughter and joy, and grown deep relationships. The gospel has been shared, and people have been coached and challenged, and have felt loved. Tables and couches represent everyday seating for informal gatherings. When we feel comfortable and welcome in someone's home, and when we gather there often, it becomes a safe and trusted place for discipleship. We can live as family when God will use our comfortable spaces, and our informal gatherings, as everyday chances for us to grow together in the gospel.

DATES, HOLIDAYS, AND VACATIONS

While living as a family occurs in everyday ways, some real risk—and often real reward—happens when we share with our spiritual family things we often reserve for our nuclear families. My parents go on double dates with other couples more often than not. They still find quality time for themselves, but they so value shared lives, of deep friendship and discipleship that occur by inviting others to go out together, that they prioritize double dates. These often occur at Winslow's, a local bistro they love and which has become a mission field for them. They frequently invite friends from Winslow's, and its owner Joe, into family holiday celebrations. With a strong belief everyone should be with loved ones for holiday meals and celebrations, my parents sacrifice time they get with their own kids and grandkids for the sake of discipleship.

Similarly, we learn more about people when we travel together than perhaps any other scenario. When Camp and Kathy joined Jess and me on a road trip to a wedding, the conversations in the car; the adventures and meals together as we explored a new city; and even the habits, values, and quirks we learned from each other helped us know and appreciate each other more deeply. Sharing dates, holidays, and vacations demands sacrifice; some moments might not even go well! (Do you split the check evenly or pay for your portions? What happens when one couple is consistently late leaving the hotel?) But even hard moments of sharing life are opportunities to check our hearts; see where we can believe or reflect the gospel more; and press us and others more deeply into relationship, grace, growth, and discipleship.

UNEXPECTED MOMENTS

I recently had a striking discipleship moment with my then-nine-year-old. After I'd calmed down from expressing some verbal frustration toward my kids, I apologized to them for my reaction and tone. Charlotte looked me in the eye and said, "Daddy, you jump to conclusions a lot." *Oof*! She's right: my impatience and desire for control can lead me to immediately assess a situation and respond the way that I think is most correct. I *do* think I'm usually right. (Don't we all?) But not always: sometimes my split-second conclusions miss key factors that should change my response. Jess and my kids know me best, and my guard is down more with them than anyone else. So they get my best . . . and worst. They see me at my most thoughtful . . . and least. I get theirs as well; we are family!

I praise God for that moment of insightful rebuke from my mini-me: He had prepared my heart and Charlotte's for the words, and rather than letting me draw snap conclusions again or defend myself (sounds silly, no, to defend myself to a child?), God brought other examples to mind, and helped me hear her well. We talked about it, I apologized to Charlotte and the rest of the family, and I'm prayerfully pursuing patience. (It's working . . . sometimes.)

101 WAYS TO MOVE FROM FAÇADE TO FAMILY

69 Plan movie nights, ball games, or hikes with your spiritual family—and do these regularly.

70 Plan an overnight trip with others—all together, just guys or just ladies, or a mix.

71 Include others in family vacations—you'll really get to know each other!

72 Watch kids while parents take a vacation—and have your spiritual family watch yours while you get away.

But discipleship opportunities often come in unexpected moments like these. We're prepared for them in "formal church times and places"—Sunday gatherings, events, or group meetings—but again, Jesus often shaped His followers through lessons taught without a moment's notice, using "on the road" examples like a grain field, or a widow's offering, or being interrupted, or being invited into someone's home (or inviting Himself into Zacchaeus's home!).

What's your response when a child (or a "less mature believer" in your mind) rebukes you, or when a neighbor points out something he noticed the previous week, or when a friend drops by unexpectedly? Maybe a harder question is whether we even pay attention to "small, mundane, everyday" things enough to see discipleship moments. Are we too consumed and fast-paced to even notice? Our attentiveness and responses to unexpected moments in our "normal" lives determine whether those become opportunities to live as family or not.

GATHERINGS, CLASSES, & MEETINGS

In discussing discipleship outside of "official church events," we cannot negate Sunday gatherings, church small groups, and other classes or meetings. But some forms of discipleship cannot occur in those settings. I've focused today on interactions that are less common for Christians in the West: we're used to forms of discipleship that occur in "official church events." But if we're honest, we know those set times and places don't give others a full view of our lives. They don't always hit on our most pressing issues or struggles. In short, they can't address all the discipleship we need. It's other times and places—like, but not limited to, those mentioned today—that fill needed gaps, and help us grow in Christ in other ways. Spiritual families pursue discipleship in planned and unplanned times and spaces, in the normal course of everyday life together.

A GROWING FAMILY

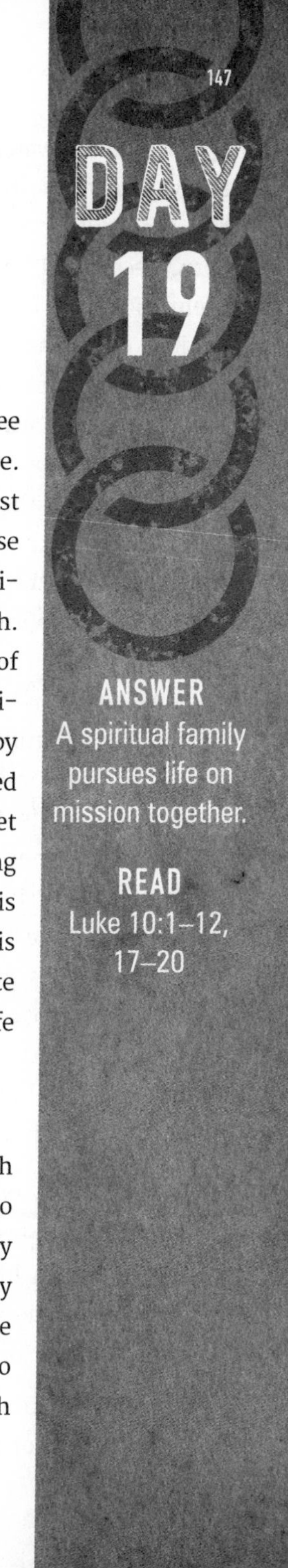

ANSWER

A spiritual family pursues life on mission together.

READ

Luke 10:1–12, 17–20

HEALTHY BEINGS REPRODUCE.

The seed of a healthy apple that grows on the tree in our backyard could produce a new apple tree. But each apple contains multiple seeds: the most fruitful apples can become a new orchard, as those multiple seeds create multiple new trees! Similarly, a mark of a healthy church family is growth. Whether by "adoption" (as already-followers of Jesus are brought into a life of worship, obedience, ministry, and mission with us) or ideally by "birth" (as not-yet-believers become involved and move from darkness into light as they meet and follow Jesus). A healthy family is a growing family, and healthy spiritual families reflect this reality in pursuing a life of mission together. This commonly happens in two ways: as we invite not-yet-believers into our spiritual family's life and as our we go out into the world together.

INVITING IN

Day 13 introduced Christian hospitality, which we saw as meaningfully including someone who doesn't belong. Church leaders can certainly help "newcomers" feel welcome on a Sunday morning, but we can forget the biggest hurdle to someone who doesn't follow Jesus: we try to welcome that person to a church building, which is a very uncomfortable first step for many!

Jess and I rewatched NBC's *The Office* recently. In one episode many Dunder-Mifflin employees unexpectedly descend on the christening of Jim and Pam's (John Krasinski and Jenna Fisher) firstborn, Cecelia. Different characters present different views of the event—Ryan (B. J. Novak) channels Karl Marx's view of religion as "opium of the masses" and Michael (Steve Carrell) imitates the godfather. Some employees are just there for the food; others to support their coworkers. All these attend the church service, but always-downtrodden Toby Flenderson (Paul Lieberstein) cannot even bring himself to enter the building. Multiple times throughout the episode, he approaches the doors only to turn away, distraught each time. Only after the service ends and the sanctuary empties does he enter. He then approaches a crucifix, looks up, and pleads sadly with God, "Why do You have to be so mean to me?"[5]

Some not-yet-believers reflect Ryan's disdain for religion, entering Sunday gatherings looking for things to mock or debate. Others are there to consume religious goods and services, or to show camaraderie for friends. For many though, shame, fear, anger, or guilt makes Sunday morning a last step back into organized religion—while some churches insist that it be the first. Instead of forcing people toward the "hardest turf," what if we invited people into our daily lives, homes, and relationships with other believers? If we create welcoming space, intentionality, and the relationships described in this book, it's a less threatening first step. And if our close spiritual family is with us in those invitations, we create everyday displays of the gospel, together.

"APOLOGETIC" LIVES, TOGETHER

Francis Schaeffer describes a church family on mission and claims that such life together is a greater defense for the gospel than logical apologetics and theological arguments, especially as the world moves increasingly into post-Christendom:

> If we are surrounded by a world which no longer believes in the concept of truth, certainly we cannot expect people to

> have any interest in whether a man's doctrine is correct or not. But Jesus did give the mark that will arrest the attention of the world, even the attention of the modern man.
>
> . . . Because every man is made in the image of God and has therefore aspirations for love. There is something that can be in every geographical climate, in every point of time, which cannot fail to arrest his attention. What is it? The love that true Christians show for each other, and not just their own party.[6]

Christians might let our guard down around other Christians, interacting in friendly, informal, and normal ways. But when with those who don't follow Jesus, we enter "project mode": interactions can become formal, goal-oriented, and awkward. Some seem to always look for ways to force Jesus into the conversation. Others avoid topics that are too deep, lest faith come up and we're asked a question we don't know how to answer or have to discuss something uncomfortable. Many followers of Jesus separate our interactions into these categories: we have "family nights" with Christians, and separately ("*seldom*-ly"?) we have "mission nights" with those who aren't. By contrast, I hope you've noticed in the stories from churches around the world how intertwined "family life" and "mission" can be. Schaeffer similarly rejects this separation: the best case for Christ (if you will) is made when those who don't follow Jesus experience the life His followers live together; the life together we've been considering throughout this book. It's through being brought into the meaningful relationship God's people have with each other, that people often taste and see that God is good.

When not-yet-believers experience the level of caring and sharing that occurs between us and participate in the openness and vulnerability of our lives, they experience Christ in us. When they see us offend each other, engage the offense honestly, and forgive each other (rather than walk away, destroy, or "ghost" each other), they see gospel on display. When they are invited into our homes (which are open and inviting), lives (which are messy but intentional), discussions (which are honest and directed toward the gospel), struggles (which are many but discussed freely because we embrace Jesus' perfection in our imperfection), burdens and joys (which respectively lead us to depend on, or celebrate, God), and even Bible studies and prayers (which are important, so let's not shy away from them when not-yet-believers are around), God often gives us opportunities to discuss truth, talk about Jesus, pray together, and share good news with friends who don't know Him.

GOING OUT

While our homes are often safer turf for not-yet-believers than a Sunday church gathering, an even more sacrificial way to live on mission is to give them "home field advantage," and meet them on their turf. Jesus sent His followers out "as sheep among wolves," and sent them out in pairs. He calls us—plural and together, not individually—salt and light in the world around us (Matt. 10:16; 5:13–16). Living on mission in the midst of an unbelieving world makes us depend on sisters and brothers: it means we take other disciples into proverbial darkness with us.

Practical and spiritual reasons exist for pursuing God's mission together: it's simply easier to share any load or responsibility than to bear it alone. In my church's work with asylum seekers, it's not uncommon for people entering the apartment complex where many refugees live to be surrounded by kids and adults alike. Some seek updates, others share needs, and still others want to say "hi" or play. Often church members go together, simply to engage with as many people as they can while making sure the specific reason for the visit can happen uninterrupted. Separately, as we follow Jesus' example, we might live out our faith in bars, college parties, homeless camps, or public forums. In the eyes of religious leaders, places like these are modern versions of first-century tax collectors' or prostitutes' homes, leper colonies, or temples of foreign gods. While religious leaders rejected these and other places of overt spiritual need, Jesus entered, because "those who are well have no need of a physician, but those who are sick. I came not to call the righteous, but sinners" (Mark 2:17). As we follow Jesus into mission, wisdom says that we need others alongside us: we can then guard each other from temptation, find the right words and responses, strengthen and encourage each other, debrief and discern the next steps together, and celebrate fruitfulness together.

The New York City ministry of Dr. Tim Keller, one of today's most prolific evangelical thinkers, was largely shaped around his unique blend of philosophical-but-winsome, gospel-centered preaching. But his early ministry, in rural Virginia, was different: "In a big town, because they like the way you preach, they will then trust you to come and share their troubles with you. In a small town . . . if they see you being wise and kind and loving, they will trust you to come and listen to your sermons. You had to spend time with them in the nursing home, in the prison, at the funeral home."[7] For most Christians, who will never step into a pulpit or lead a church, this is even more poignant.

SENDING FAMILY MEMBERS IS HARD

An overt step in living on mission together is sending some spiritual family members to new mission fields to live life together and display and declare the gospel there, or to start a new church in that new mission field. Sending family members away is hard and seems contrary to the whole impulse of this book. You've read, "Be more devoted, go deeper, and intertwine your lives increasingly." Sending seems to say the opposite: "Go away!" But if my children never leave the nest—to, say, pursue education, travel the world, or start a family of their own—I've actually parented them poorly. If they are unable to exist and form their own families as they enter adulthood, and to then adopt or birth offspring of their own, Jess and I have not equipped them to fulfill God's first positive command in the Bible: "Be fruitful and multiply" (Gen. 1:28). I cannot currently imagine my kids leaving the house—they are still years away—but part of my role during those years is preparing them to send them into the lives God has for them. Our spiritual families are similar: part of our role is training and sending some to start new families.

I've worked with dozens of church planters over the past half decade, and those who start churches with a strong core team of committed Christ-followers have an easier time than those who go alone. A goal of the Soma Family, the organization my church is part of, is seeing at least one "missional community"—or whatever title a spiritual family living on mission embraces; "a rose by any other name would smell as sweet"[8]—started per one thousand people across North America and beyond. Accomplishing this takes sacrifice and intentionality and requires lots of spiritual families to send members out. Some spiritual siblings must be willing to be seeds God will use to plant new, spiritual orchards.

A CHRISTIAN FAMILY IS A MISSIONARY FAMILY

For more on today's topic, Bob Roberts Jr. and I wrote *A Field Guide for Everyday Mission*, which considers theological and practical elements of Christians living on mission in our day to day lives.

101 WAYS TO MOVE FROM FAÇADE TO FAMILY

73 Treat people like family who aren't yet part of God's family: we share one Creator and are made in His image—many of these "101 ways" apply to all people, whether Christian or not.

74 Commit to shared mission: when we pursue a "people group" together, we share prayer, accountability, ideas, and mission with our spiritual siblings.

75 Invite non-Christians into your spiritual family's events: when nonbelievers see our crazy life together, God often opens doors to explain the gospel.

76 Go into darkness together: join other spiritual siblings in building relationships, declaring the gospel, remaining "unstained" from the world, and being "light in darkness."

British preacher Charles Spurgeon famously said, "Every Christian . . . is either a missionary or an impostor. Recollect that you are either trying to spread abroad the kingdom of Christ, or else you do not love him at all. It cannot be that there is a high appreciation of Jesus, and a totally silent tongue about him . . . that man who says, 'I believe in Jesus,' but does not think enough of Jesus ever to tell another about him, by mouth, or pen, or tract, is an impostor."[9]

When we live out God's design for His spiritual family, we necessarily pursue His mission. That mission happens in the context of everyday lives, as we invite in and as we go out. And that mission happens best when it is shared with spiritual sisters and brothers, pursuing God's mission together. Are we willing to lay down our comfort, invite not-yet-believers onto our turf, and humbly enter theirs? Are we willing to be—or send out—seeds of a new, spiritual orchard? By God's grace and through the power of the Spirit, healthy Christians make new Christians, together.

WEEK FOUR IN ACTION

The last day of each week you will read how churches across the world live as a family and will discuss this week's content with others. As you discuss the questions, be honest with yourself and others, and let them speak truth in love, as you put this book into practice together.

LIVING AS FAMILY: TRINITY MINSTER, NARAGUTA, NIGERIA

The church bell rang about 9:00 a.m., a very odd hour. As it tolled in the distance, an eerie silence filled our house. We knew all was not well. I lived in a compound of eight double rooms, housing eight different families. The women dropped what they were doing, and I joined a group from my compound for the six-minute walk to the church. A vehicle was parked at one entrance and a coffin was being carried in. We joined the palpable sorrow and uncontrollable sobbing, and women had to be led away as people went to the bereaved family to offer condolences. But at the end of his funeral sermon, the pastor requested people *not* to bring any more cooked food to the house of the bereaved because there was so much that the foods were beginning to go bad. He asked people to support the family in any other way. As months rolled by, families rallied around to help the children cope with the passing of their father and ensured that school fees for the five children were all paid.

The church life, among most Christians in northern Nigeria, has always been groups of people knit together by the love of Jesus Christ irrespective of denominations. Living in this part of the country, where majority of the people are Muslims and discrimination can be intense, care for one another is an intrinsic part of the community life.

I owe my education at Baptist High School in Jos, Nigeria, to my church in Tudun Wada, Kaduna. My father didn't send me to a secondary school because he had just divorced my mum and no one else could babysit my sisters, who were barely two and four years old. I stayed home for two years. Then, when new admission forms arrived, our pastor handed me one and asked me to complete it and bring it back to him. There was no way my father would allow me to go, but I reluctantly collected the form, filled it out, and sent it back. My father rarely went to church anyway, so I doubted the pastor knew my father

101 WAYS TO MOVE FROM FAÇADE TO FAMILY

77 Don't limit certain gatherings to Christians and others to non-Christians. Integrate these groups and pray that God will open doors to the gospel.

78 Host events: Summer barbecues, community gardens, progressive dinners—things like these offer people opportunities to enter others' lives.

79 Bless others: be the first to show up. Be generous with gifts or food. Be quick to repent and offer forgiveness. And explain why.

80 Designate a "ministry budget": set aside monthly spending for mission and ministry. Use it. It can be small; the fact it's there matters!

or could convince him to let me go. A week later, the pastor told me the entrance examination was coming up and urged me to try hard at the exam. I did the best I could on short notice. Weeks went by, then one Sunday the pastor handed me an admission letter!

I will never know if the pastor spoke to my father, but I was shocked when my father asked me to get ready to go to school. When he complained bitterly about lacking money to buy the school's requirements (a metal box, shoes, a bucket, bedsheets, and a mattress), I reached out to my mother for help. Eventually only my father paid, but only part of my first term fees. The principal of Musa Bawa, who was also a pastor, realised the challenge I faced and let me do work in the school to offset my fees and enable me to graduate. I came to realise, much later, that the church assisted many of us young men and women, working with our parents to make sure we were educated.

The church has always been the big family for so many of us.

Ven. Hassan John

"WHEN & WHERE" QUESTIONS TO DISCUSS

- [ ] **GENERAL**: What impacted you most this week? What was new, convicting, difficult, or confusing? What biblical truths do you need others to remind you of, in love?
- [ ] **GENERAL**: Given this week's content, what people, things, or ideas would you say you're most "devoted" to? How "devoted" are you to God's people and their spiritual growth?
- [ ] **DAY 16**: Which element—God's Word, God's people, whole-life worship, or God's mission—are you most devoted to, and how does that look? Which are you least, and why?
- [ ] **DAY 16**: How might it look to pursue devotion to God's Word, God's people, whole-life worship, and God's mission that reflects the first-century church? What would it take, and how would others need to help you pursue that?

- ☐ **DAY 17:** What image of yourself do you portray to others, and what happens when it breaks down? How is Jesus good news to your imperfections, and how does His gospel free you to be honest with Him and others?

- ☐ **DAY 17:** What would it take to prioritize relationship, speaking and listening, and location over busyness and our own agendas? What would it take, and how would others need to help you pursue that?

- ☐ **DAY 18:** Who in your life are you closest to, and how well do they honestly know you? What areas are "off limits" from them, and why? What would it take, to pursue full "known-ness" with others, through whole-life discipleship?

- ☐ **DAY 18:** What truths of God empower us to open our everyday rhythms, homes, dates, holidays, vacations, and unexpected moments to others? How might God grow our knowledge and love for Him and others by doing so?

- ☐ **DAY 19:** What priority does your close spiritual family put on God's mission? How can you join in prayer and practice to support each other to pursue the great commission?

- ☐ **DAY 19:** How does (or could) your close spiritual family proactively live on mission together by "inviting in"? How do (or could) you do this by "going out"?

- ☐ **GENERAL:** This week introduced several examples of "whens" and "wheres" God's people live as a spiritual family. Some apply to your situation; others might not. What other ways and places can you live like a spiritual family with others? What could you change, add, and engage so this week's content fits your context?

- ☐ **GENERAL:** Look over this week's "101 Ways." What else could you do, per your own gifting, spiritual family, and mission field, to live as God's family? Post ideas with the hashtag, #genuine community.

WEEK FIVE

HOW DO WE START?

Be doers of the word, and not hearers only,
deceiving yourselves. . . .
So also faith by itself, if it does not have works, is dead.
But someone will say, "You have faith and I have works."
Show me your faith apart from your works, and I will
show you my faith by my works. (James 1:22; 2:17–18)

THIS BOOK IS *NOT* THE BIBLE . . .

. . . but I hope you'll agree that the content you've read, discussed, and started practicing over the past twenty days are *biblical*. I tried to reflect the heart, charge, and invitation of God and the way He created His children to operate, together, for His glory. Even if some examples or practices don't exactly apply to your situation, the principles you have read start with, and point toward, God's design for His people—His spiritual family.

The danger in writing a "Field Guide"-type book—one that invites participation, gives examples, and tries to move from heart-level worship and head-level theology into hands-level practice—is creating a checklist. It can be seen as guilt-inspiring duties that readers cannot achieve. But throughout the Bible, God consistently invites His people to move beyond knowledge to joyful obedience. Our faith is proven when our belief overflows into action and lifestyle. It's only as internal belief turns to eternal fruit that Jesus' good news is displayed and declared. As our choices and goals change, we can be increasingly certain that our heart has changed. Of course, we can fake it—humans are good at that! But the consistent theme throughout the Bible is captured in James 2: faith without works is dead.

Adam and Eve's first sin was an act of rebellion against God's authority; a declaration that they knew better than Him. God gave Moses the Ten Commandments not to oppress Israel but to help them know how His "display community"[1] could reflect their faith and belief to each other and other nations. The Old Testament deems Israel's and Judah's kings "good" or "bad" primarily based on whether or not they led their subjects toward or away from worshiping God through obeying His law. John the Baptist refused to baptize individuals whose heads were full of knowledge but whose lives did not "bear fruit in keeping with repentance" (Matt. 3:8). Jesus charged His disciples, "If you love me, you will keep my commandments" (John 14:15). The New Testament authors discuss the change of heart that comes from following Jesus, and all tell readers what their lives and relationships look like as a result of that heart change. Again, Jesus' brother James summarizes this biblical theme: "I will show you my faith by my works."

Modern examples of living out God's commands have already filled the pages of this book. But Week Five takes a few final steps into putting the theory and theology of "church as family" into everyday practice. What does modern-day obedience look like? How do we go from belief to action? This week we give some tangible first steps to answering a final question, "How do we start?"

ANSWER
We start by knowing & applying the gospel.

READ
1 Corinthians 15:1–5

A WHOLE-LIFE GOSPEL

"IF JESUS IS REAL, HE SHOULD MATTER TO ALL OF LIFE."

That epiphany hit me like a ton of bricks as I walked across my university campus. It now seems like an obvious thought for a follower of Jesus (especially one who was two years into a ministry job, as I was!). But that sunny afternoon in my third year of studies was the first time God opened my eyes to see the full impact of His good news. I had been raised in a religious culture; I was a "good kid" through high school and a leader in my youth group.

I had taught Bible stories. God had used me as a vessel to lead other people to Him. But I don't think I truly knew Him—at least, not in a way that mattered to my actual life. For two years I lived a dual life, on one hand a student pastor and on the other pursuing some stereotypical vices of American university students. But that day I knew something must change.

TWO-THIRDS OF THE GOSPEL

Many followers of Jesus have a similar story: with or without a religious upbringing, and however God drew you to Himself through the sacrificial victory of Jesus, there are parts of our lives that Jesus hasn't yet changed. There are aspects in each of us that are being grown, refined, and sanctified. The good news of Jesus hasn't yet mattered to everything in your life. Moment of honesty: I get frustrated reading the apostle John at times. In some of his writing it seems like Jesus called John to Himself and John instantly became perfect. ("No one who abides in him keeps on sinning," 1 John 3:6. *Ouch*!) By comparison, do I ever resonate with the apostle Paul's journey of sanctification? ("For I do not do the good I want, but the evil I do not want is what I keep on doing," Rom. 7:19—anyone else!) In today's reading from 1 Corinthians, Paul draws us back to the gospel. That Christ lived, died, rose, was buried, was raised, ascended, and will one day return is the central truth that is "of first importance" to Jesus' followers (15:3).

Most of us agree: "Of course Jesus is important!" But many of us disconnect that "first importance" belief from our daily activities. In other words, many followers of Jesus only believe two-thirds of the gospel—and if we're going to see how to actually live in the relationship God invites us into, we must realize our need for that missing, final one-third.

The two-thirds gospel can be summarized by saying, a little tongue-in-cheek, that the gospel is a past event that greatly benefits my future. It's a past event, in that we believe Jesus really lived a perfect life, really died a substitutionary death for our sins, really rose as the victorious conqueror of eternal death and separation, and really ascended as our advocate to the Father. Further, there was a moment in every Christian's past that we didn't believe that, then another moment when we finally did. That's the "past" one-third of the gospel: Jesus lived in history past, and I met Him in my personal past.

We also believe a future reality of the gospel: because of Jesus' past work, my future benefits greatly! "You don't have to go to hell," the evangelist preaches, "you get to go to heaven instead!" Because of Jesus' past work, we look forward to glorified perfection. We get a restored relationship with God. Our eternity is secure; *we get God, forever*! That is the "future" reality of the gospel: the second-third.

Lest we swing the pendulum too far, we pause and celebrate: the gospel *is* a past reality, and it *is* a future reality! We saw this in Paul's words today: we "received" the gospel (past tense), and we "are being saved, if [we] hold fast to the word" (the grammar indicates a continual move toward our future, perfected state). But while these two-thirds of the gospel are true and glorious, they're incomplete: we also "stand" in "the gospel I preached to you": standing is a present tense activity (1 Cor. 15:1–3). Paul pens similar sentiments throughout the New Testament. For example, "In [the gospel] the righteousness of God is revealed from faith [past] for faith [future], as it is written, 'The righteous shall live by faith' [present]" (Rom. 1:17). The gospel doesn't just matter for our past and future; it matters for every moment of our *present* existence too: every decision, struggle, relationship, thought, word, goal, everything. *If Jesus is real, He should matter to all of life!*

While the past and future "thirds" of the gospel matter deeply, it's the present "third" that helps us put this book into practice. The gospel is the right starting point and right goal of this devoted life to God and to each other.

OUR STARTING POINT

In truth, there are many motivations for pursuing deeper relationships with fewer Christians. Some people have aversions to large crowds. Others are comfortable with the few Christian friends they already have. Church leaders could use commitment to manipulate people from leaving a church, or to abdicate some of their own calling ("If everyone is in deep relationship, I don't have to shepherd as much"). There are problems with these and other poor motivations. And none will sufficiently sustain us over the long haul; if our friends require too much of us, or if people keep leaving a church, for example, we replace our pursuit of this relational depth with something else we feel might work better. Instead of these and other false and fading motivations, the good news of Jesus is the best motive for living as spiritual siblings. When we increasingly drink from the beautiful, deep well of Christ, He sustains our pursuit, and as His truth and Spirit take deeper root in our hearts—He concurrently drives us toward deeper relationships.

After all, we can only enter God's family through Jesus' death and resurrection in the first place! That same gospel helps us view each other as spiritual siblings. Jesus' example and teachings drive us to overcome our differences, value other perspectives, and pursue "the other"—other politics, ethnicities, or generations, and so forth—and to tear down every dividing wall between God's people. The good news of a better kingdom than our own frees us to let down façades and become open and vulnerable—with our homes, possessions, struggles, and lives. As we rely on Jesus' perfection, He frees us to embrace and display our imperfection!

On and on we could go. "For all the promises of God find their Yes in him [Jesus Christ]" (2 Cor. 1:20). In the gospel we find the basis of unconditional love for hard people, a willingness to accept and learn from children and "less mature" believers, and the desire and power to speak truth in love together. Jesus was the ultimate model of each "one another" command; He is the Chief Shepherd who empowers us to shepherd each other; He perfectly invited us in, sacrificed most for us, came to earth as the truest fulfillment of God's mission, and so much more. His Spirit fills us, empowers us, and sends us into that same world with one right motive. As we increasingly believe His good news in every facet of our present life, we increasingly display and declare that good news into others' lives. The gospel is our one sustaining message and our one sustaining motive to live as family.

OUR RIGHT GOAL

As many poor motives exist for living as family, there are also many poor goals for that endeavor—each of which can let us down. Some of us love the self-satisfaction of "helping a lightbulb come on" in someone's realization of new spiritual truth—and become frustrated when months go by without any new "aha" moments. Others take pride in our obedience—and feel guilty when we feel we fail God. Some church leaders rest on "familial relationships" as a purer form of church and hope it will more quickly mitigate sin. Holiness is a great goal, but no method or ministry strategy is a silver bullet to eradicate sin.

Just as the gospel is the only sustainable motive, it is the only sustainable goal. We saw that the goal of "speaking the truth in love" is that God's people "grow up in every way into him who is the head, into Christ," so God's body "builds itself up in love," together (Eph. 4:15–16). Only a deep, unconditional pursuit of others, motivated by Jesus' deep, unconditional pursuit of us, drives us deeply into others' lives. Only His devotion to us sustains our devotion to others. "We love because He first loved us" (1 John 4:19). Jesus says that love, for God and others, fulfills God's law. God the Spirit awakens the love for Him and for others in us and drives us to pursue their thriving to the same degree we pursue our own. Our growth in maturity, faithfulness, holiness, and sanctification together is our goal—and that only starts, continues, and ends with the gospel. Jesus, and the past, present, and future aspects of his good news, are our right motivation and goal.

101 WAYS TO MOVE FROM FAÇADE TO FAMILY

81 Know the Bible. The more you dwell with God and know Him, the better you can share biblical truth together.

82 Listen "under the surface" to people—for longings, disappointments, pains, and hopes.

83 Address issues early; do not let bitterness grow; "keep short accounts" with others. Get everything in the light, ASAP!

84 Mourn together biblically: grieve, pray, and care—in miscarriages, loss of parents or children, unexpected job transitions, or even "minor" setbacks.

OUR RIGHT MESSAGE

As the gospel is our right starting point and right goal, it's also our right message. In sending Christ as Messiah, God reversed the curse of sin, ushered in a new kingdom, promised restoration for all brokenness, and assures us that He is better than anything else in life. Fighting to increasingly believe this and fighting for our spiritual siblings to increasingly believe this, is the primary "truth in love" we speak. God's truth offers refreshment and can pour out of us into others, as we hear and share each other's stories, struggles, needs, and idols.

In Jesus, God offers joy to the joyless, hope to the hopeless, companionship to the lonely, freedom to the oppressed, answers to the questioner, belonging to those who are lost, love to the rejected, and so much more! This is not just true at the beginning of our Christian life, although one of those truths may have been what made the gospel sound like truly "good news" to you. It is also true for each of God's children, as we all keep growing up in Christ.

Living as a devoted spiritual family starts with increasingly realizing how deep the gospel of God goes, that there is no better motive or goal than Jesus. Living as a devoted spiritual family also starts with increasingly embracing the whole-life application of that gospel. Resting in the gospel frees us to let down our façades and be honest with our beauty and warts, our strengths and our needs: if we're fully known by God and still fully loved, we can allow others to know and love us too. Being fully approved by God through the blood of His Son frees us from needing to prove ourselves to others. As we start applying the gospel to our present lives, we can also apply it to each other, helping others see Jesus' invitation to a better identity, story, hope, better savior, than whatever someone currently finds her or his identity, hope, and redemption in.

Putting the past twenty days into practice starts with our own head and heart. It starts with believing the past, present, and future gospel. It starts with believing that gospel is "of first importance" as our starting point and end goal for this living as family. And it starts with increasingly speaking the gospel as our primary message. Living as family starts with believing that if Jesus is real, He should matter to all of life!

"WELCOME" SIGNS

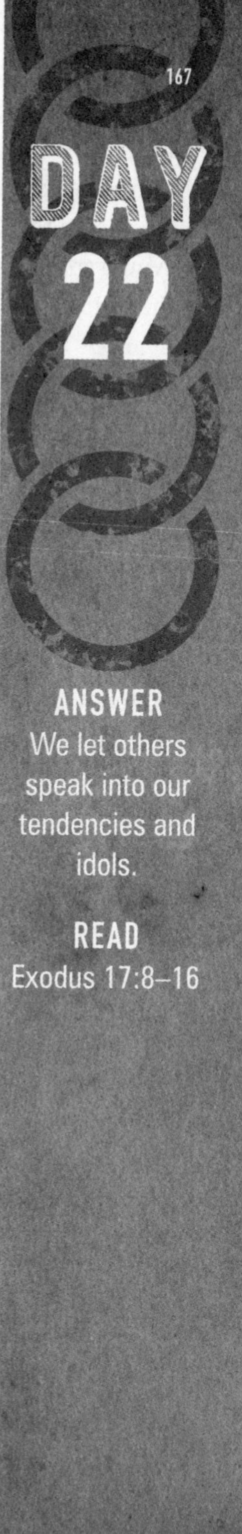

"WHAT ARE YOU BAD AT?"

Our church planting residency's written application asks about strengths, but we save this second question for in-person interviews. No one likes to admit things we're bad at! As we prepare for job interviews, we "put our best foot forward" and "turn our weaknesses into strengths." Honestly, residency applicants' specific answers to this question—"What things are you bad at?"—are often less important than how the applicant responds.

Some chuckle and admit their flaws sheepishly, but fairly quickly. That's the kind of honest response I hope for. But it's not the one I always hear. Some applicants respond with shame or disparagement; I had to stop one and encourage him, as his list of weaknesses continued growing. While I appreciate the humility and self-awareness, they can at times display distrust toward God—that His forgiveness didn't cover their guilt; that His goodness doesn't free them from shame; that their confidence rises and falls based on what they do (and cannot do), more than what God has done and is doing in and through them. But when asked what they are bad at, some applicants become defensive or evasive ("Why would you ask that?" one clipped back); others do not know ("Uh . . . hmm . . . it's hard to say . . . "). Inability to admit weakness—or unawareness it might exist—is often a yellow flag, sometimes ending an applicant's process.

A theme through this book is that Christians need each other. A devoted spiritual family needs each other practically: we share each other's loads, help and serve each other, give and receive together. At various times we need each other emotionally (like entering each other's celebrations and grief), financially (like meeting needs), socially (like talking to someone or simply hanging out), mentally (like wrestling with a problem or question). But we always need each other spiritually. Even in these other areas of need, we need the prayers, encouragement, exhortation, rebuke, support, love, care, and godliness we lack. We need each other's areas of maturity to help grow our areas of immaturity.

To receive from each other spiritually, we have to admit that we're not good at everything. Pursuing the deep relationships God has for us means letting God develop our willingness to admit needs, and to let others into every facet of our lives to meet those needs. In the do-it-yourself, individualistic, image-centric, and polite culture of our societies and churches, this may be the biggest hurdle to overcome.

"DO NOT ENTER"

Do you ever try to sneak a peek "behind the scenes"? (Or is that just me?) Whether in theme parks, museums, office buildings, or even grocery stores, I'm drawn to anything "off-limits," "employees only" hallways, backstage doors, or "do not enter" signs. I know nothing intriguing is usually behind those signs (mostly dirty broom closets or florescent-lit employee break rooms) but I'm still drawn to them, in the off chance that I might glimpse how something works—or per Day 17, to see "the man behind the curtain."

My friend Jimmy grew up in Florida and went to Walt Disney World on a regular basis; once, he and his family participated in behind-the-scenes tours. I salivated as Jimmy once described to me the network of tunnels, hidden doors, operations and technology that exist, sometimes hidden in plain sight and often underneath the theme park. It seems like the ultimate "behind the scenes" experience!

Each of us has areas of our lives we keep hidden like Disney's secrets. We portray the "happy theme park version" of ourselves, where the proverbial brightly colored buildings and characters of our lives look polished and together. To accomplish this, we hide weaknesses, faults, and imperfections. We put up "do not enter" signs on some areas of our lives. Some areas are common; others are specific to each of us. We've already mentioned that we all have areas of Christian belief, worship, and practice where God has provided growth and maturity. But are we willing to let others into the areas we're uniquely *not* mature? We all admit we're imperfect in general, but can we go deeper and admit specific areas of struggle, sin, weakness, and need?

I share my own spiritual journey, including my ongoing struggles, with women and men in my group and even in sermons, on a regular basis (my most common wrestles are with lust and control, and at times, impatience). I don't share these because I'm proud of them, or to look holy because I'm willing to admit them. Letting others in is hard, but I know that if others are aware of my weaknesses, they can be on the lookout with me, guarding me against temptation and pointing out areas of my life where sin seems to rear its ugly head. Letting others into my weaknesses is also risky. In Lin-Manuel Miranda's hit musical *Hamilton*, the protagonist admits dalliance to his "frenemy" Aaron Burr, then asks, "How do I know you won't use this against me the next time we go toe to toe?" Burr responds ominously, "Alexander, rumors only grow. And we both know what we know."

Fear of a similar response often leads us to hide sin. And in the musical, Hamilton's honesty leads to his undoing. But in my experience, this level of honesty instead bolsters my battle for holiness: if people know my brokenness in more latent times, I can reach out without surprising them in moments where it is more overt. We each have areas of immaturity, imperfection, sin, unwisdom, and need. What's at risk to admit your brokeness to others? What's at risk to take yourself off the pedestal you place yourself on (rather than seeing it crash down one day) and form an army to join your fight against sin and for holiness as you also join theirs?

THE HIDDEN TRIFECTA

If you're looking for a first area of life to let people see, maybe you and your spiritual siblings can start with a common "off-limits" areas in Christian adults' lives. The "trifecta" that stays nearly universally hidden involves finances, marriage or singleness, and parenting.

Money

Even though Jesus offers more teaching and caution on money than any other topic except the kingdom of God, our finances are hidden behind our lives' locked doors. Maybe we actually believe Jesus when He says, "Where your treasure is, there your heart will be also" (Matt. 6:21)—so we don't want others to see what people, things, habits, or hobbies truly have our hearts. Eric and Allie's group has walked together for years, and they choose to combat financial temptation by having an "open books" policy: each family knows how much the others make and each can ask at any time about each other's spending, saving, investing, and giving. This may seem extreme, but it's effective in bringing anything hidden into the light.

Marriage or Singleness

Marriage—which displays the spiritual relationship between Jesus and the Church—is a consistent source of counseling conversations. Some unmarried people secretly idolize or despise it or simply don't feel they can discuss it. Some married people only seek help when things reach a breaking point or when one spouse forces the other to admit they need help. If Satan seeks to kill and destroy, and consistently works against godly things like unity, then everything from Christian divorce statistics to stories we know or have lived, to temptations we each face, point to marriage and singleness as key battle grounds for spiritual attack. But instead of seeking help, many single people and couples hide the idols, temptations, and fissures, and try to fight God's enemy alone. Jess and I have celebrated multiple single people walking together in friendship and dating relationships, pursuing pointed conversations and fighting temptation together. We have also seen multiple couples reach out to trusted sisters and brothers early in a conflict, so issues can heal before they grow or explode.

Parenting

Jess and I often tell expectant couples in our church (and oh, there have been many over the years) that parenting is one of the most divisive topics in Christianity. Well before parents ask for it, people are ready to dish out sage advice. (We're all experts if we try one thing, one time, with one kid, and it works, right?) Parents' responses of silence and scowls communicate that these topics are "off-limits." While self-appointed counselors could grow in showing more grace, parents can also pursue experienced friends, rather than feeling everything is up to them! From sleep training to schooling choices to discipline to discipleship and more, parents plant hedges around their decisions—no one seems allowed to comment on choices.

QUESTIONS AND ANSWERS

Reformer John Calvin famously wrote, "The human mind is, so to speak, a perpetual forge of idols."[2] We let others in when we admit this, ask God for a desire to fight those idols, and ask for help. Of course, it would be easier if others invited us into their brokenness first—it's less risky to follow than to lead. But if the gospel is our best motivator (see yesterday), God can give us the Spirit-led boldness we need to go first.

If this degree of honesty is new for your spiritual family, perhaps start with questions. Ask, for example, "How do you feel when . . . ?", "What are you struggling with?", or "What don't we know about you that we should?" Alternatively, start with answers: in addition to sharing and speaking into each other's stories, practice applying God's truth to hypothetical situations—and as you grow comfortable and confident, graciously do the same with one another. Appendices B and C offer "Question and Answer" tools to help this process.

The first time a group "confess[es] your sins to one another and pray[s] for one another" is weird (James 5:16). You'll have to practice being "quick to hear [and] slow to speak" (James 1:19). You'll have to trust that "faithful are the wounds of a friend" (Prov. 27:6). You'll need to grow in "draw[ing] out . . . the purpose in a man's heart [that] is like deep water" (Prov. 20:5). And you might even have to walk through the process Jesus outlines when a sister or "brother sins against you" (Matt. 18:15). But God promises these are good pursuits.

In Exodus 17, Moses oversees Israel from a hill as they battle Amalek. "Whenever Moses held up his hand, Israel prevailed, and whenever he lowered his hand, Amalek prevailed. But Moses's hands grew weary, so they took a stone and put it under him, and he sat on it, while Aaron and Hur held up his hands, one on one side, and the other on the other side. So his hands were steady until

101 WAYS TO MOVE FROM FAÇADE TO FAMILY

85 Honor each other's preferences: when conflict arises over preferences, humbly defer and celebrate your differences (see Rom. 14).

86 Ask questions in potential unwisdom: when conflict arises over matters of wisdom, ask questions and offer warnings—don't rebuke or discipline if it's not sin!

87 Rebuke others' sin, in love: when someone does sin and doesn't see it, the Bible helps us rebuke, in relational trust and prayerful love.

88 Address conflict biblically: when you face sin, walk through Matthew 18:15–20—Christians often ignore this, but God shows us exactly what to do!

the going down of the sun. And Joshua overwhelmed Amalek and his people with the sword" (vv. 11–13). At times in our fights for holiness, we each feel like Moses: like we're winning at times but losing at others. We all grow weary—but rather than giving up, a close spiritual family is our "Aaron and Hur," entering our battle with us, holding our arms, and helping us fight. And we get to be Aaron or Hur for them. This is true devotion and familial relationship. But it happens when we let others into our weakness, sin, and need; remove the "do not enter" signs; and ask for help.

DAY 23

ANSWER
We bring whatever we have for the good of His body.

READ
1 Corinthians 14:26–33

ONE SMALL STEP FOR MAN . . .

"HOW DO YOU EAT AN ELEPHANT?"

As the saying quips, the only way to tackle such a daunting task is "one bite at a time." For some readers, the principles, example, and suggestions in the book so far seem overwhelming. Today's goal is to free you from having everything all together, from figuring out every nuance of this life together that God calls His people to, and from feeling like you have to know every step before you start down this path. No one has this fully figured out; everyone who tries to live as family has "wins" and "misses"—again, even spiritual family is messy this side of eternity!

But from ancient Chinese proverbs ("The journey of a thousand miles begins with a single step") to the moon landing ("One small step for man; one giant leap for mankind") to any new endeavor we pursue, part of actually making this happen (which is this week's focus), is simply *making it happen*! With "the word of Christ dwelling in [us] richly" (Col. 3:16) and "the Spirit help[ing] us in our weakness" (Rom. 8:26), we can rest in the truths of God we've seen over the past five weeks. And with confidence in our Father, we can take a first step. No matter how small it seems, let's offer our gifts and passions to each other as acts of worship to God. Let's prayerfully invite a few others to join us and take the first bite of that elephant. Today considers what this first step might look like: it starts with everyone bringing whatever they have to the table.

A SPIRITUAL POTLUCK

Like many church groups across the world, ours eats together often. Some weeks, one family brings dinner; another week, a few university students join forces to do so. We've had theme nights; $5 pizza nights; nights where people couldn't choke down the meal that was brought; and several nights of enjoying delicious meals. We've eaten food from each other's cultures and favorite dishes from our childhoods, and each Valentine's Day we all head to Chadra, the neighborhood Mediterranean bistro, to dine out together. Our meals have looked different, week to week.

But many peoples' favorite nights over the years have been potluck nights: you never know what you're going to get! Each time we move down the line of plates and pots, we can tell that some dishes were meticulously prepared (Ava, then a student, once made delicious empanadas upon returning from a semester in Argentina), while others were hastily picked up on the way over (Dan, also a student, once brought green beans and eggs!). Some people spent a fair bit of money on their dish (at some points, our group involved around forty people), and other times people couldn't afford to contribute. But guess what? Every week, everyone who walked into the house was nourished by whatever tasty food had been offered; and everyone who walked into the house was received, no matter how much or how little they were able to bring.

A potluck is a tangible picture of what God has His people do together. Today's reading from 1 Corinthians describes a "spiritual potluck" of sorts. "When you come together, each one has a hymn, a lesson, a revelation, a tongue, or an interpretation. Let all things be done for building up" (14:26). We may think it strange that the New Testament gives us very few glimpses of first-century "Sunday worship services." I believe this is precisely because of what the Bible instead *does* show us: the church—God's people—was together so often, living their devoted lives together and discipling each other so informally that their discipleship involved far more than "weekly worship services" like ours today. Further, the experience most Christians today have of "church" would have worked against the picture we see in 1 Corinthians 14: instead of an audience mostly receiving from a few people on a stage, and singing a few songs in a "worship set," the apostle Paul's rare picture of an early Christian church gathering instead shows a picture of "each one" contributing! Everyone brought their proverbial dish to the spiritual potluck: one brought a song, another a teaching, yet another something God had taught them or impressed upon them, and a few others might have spoken in tongues or interpreted.

INVOLVING EVERYONE

Church leaders might need to consider how our church gatherings reflect first-century worship, or what to do if the past generation's church-growth movement have made this kind of gathering impossible. But as everyday Christians pursuing deep relationships with our sisters and brothers, we might start with creating a space for everyone to bring whatever God has given them to the table. While these relationships will ideally, increasingly occur in the informal course of our everyday lives, a first step might be modeling it with a weekly time together. But what could that time look like?

Soma Communities in Tacoma, Washington, was an early voice in the modern "missional community" movement. They explain their group meetings in the following way: "A missional community is NOT primarily a small group, a Bible study, a support group, a social activist group, or a weekly meeting." But, as Soma Tacoma and others in our family of churches teach, they *do* stay small—so that everyone can know each other's stories and be involved in discipling each other. They *do* study the Bible—but in a way that drives everyone gathered to ask questions of God's perfect Word rather than primarily what a preacher imperfectly said about it. They *do* care for each other—members specifically use their gifts, resources, and perspectives for each other's needs and growth. They *do* live on mission together—most often committed to a specific geography, organization, or group of people, and/or supporting each other's callings. And they *do* meet regularly—often more than weekly, and different meetings involve different aspects of life together described in this paragraph.

In my church, some groups—especially when new—followed a monthly rhythm to develop new habits of holistic discipleship: they'd have two weeks each month more focused on prayer and discussing what they were learning from the Bible ("up" weeks, if you will). One of the in-between weeks was more "one another" focused: building relationships, caring for each other, and meeting various needs (an "in" week). And the final week was overtly dedicated to mission: praying and sharing celebrations and needs in displaying and declaring the gospel, planning, or serving together with people they regularly engaged (an "out" week). Other groups, or groups in other seasons, pursue a less structured approach but still make sure they address these multiple facets of discipleship and life together over the course of several months' meetings. And the majority of people in our groups are in the lives of at least a few other group members multiple times each week between meetings too, where relationships and discipleship continue informally.

EVERY GROUP CAN PURSUE THIS!

My church is just one example. Different Soma churches across the world put these principles into practices in dozens of different ways—some have shared examples from their churches in the pages of this book. Soma is not the only family of churches who calls God's people to this level of devotion, mutual discipleship, and life together. And "missional communities" are not the only type of group that can pursue this lifestyle: any small group, home group, life group, house church, class, or even just "church"—and even groups with no moniker at all—*can* pursue these elements. As you might guess, my conviction is that they *must* do so!

At a recent gathering of church planting trainers hosted by SEND Institute's Daniel Yang and Jeff Christopherson, one projection for the future of the North American church was that it will move "from Sunday-centric to Christ's body." Christopherson explains, "The Body of Christ now has an opportunity to express itself beyond the required machinery of Sundays as it forms an interdependent spiritual family in full view of a lonely and longing community."[3] Three commonalities Christians who want this depth of relationship share are that they value different Christians' giftings,[4] they prioritize equipping everyday Christians to thrive in those giftings and in turn equip others,[5] and they encourage peer-to-peer discipleship, in formal and informal ways in everyday life.[6]

FORM A GROUP, AND GO!

One Sunday afternoon, Jess and I went to a local garden center to buy a blackberry bush for our front porch. After picking up some flowers and fruitlessly searching the massive greenhouses for the right bushes, we finally asked the owner where they were. After pointing us in the right direction, he called after us, "Make sure you get two bushes, and make sure they're two different varieties."

101 WAYS TO MOVE FROM FAÇADE TO FAMILY

89 Celebrate your spiritual family's birthdays—to the same degree as a close nuclear family member. (Try anniversaries too!)

90 Invite your spiritual siblings to own birthday celebrations (your kids' too), like you would a close nuclear family member.

91 Celebrate holidays together: make sure no one spends Thanksgiving or Christmas Eve alone, for example.

92 Find other reasons to celebrate—one couple threw a one hundred-year birthday party for their house, just to get people together.

"*Different* varieties?" we asked, thinking we'd heard him wrong. "Yes," he replied, "you need two so that they can cross pollinate, and when they do, the strengths of the different varieties will make both of them stronger." Who knew how deeply God wove the principle of needing others, and especially others who are different from ourselves, into the fabric of His creation?

After describing what a devoted spiritual family can look like for nearly five weeks, today's invitation is to take that first bite of the elephant! Prayerfully pursue God's timing and a diverse collection of perspectives, then commit to each other for a number of months. Start getting to know each other, start meeting together regularly (both formally and informally), and simply start taking steps to live out this life, together. Help each other, encourage each other, and live out the other "one anothers" even as it relates to your shared attempt at living as family!

Each person is stronger as you all glean from your shared experience, and you'll all grow in different ways as you all share strengths in different areas of faith and discipleship. Your love and devotion for each other will continue growing over time as you all bring your gifts, passions, and possessions together for the common good and the glory of God. Value each other, help each other thrive, share all you have freely for the sake of others, and receive deeply from what others have. Month by month, and year by year, as you boldly, sacrificially pursue this life together, you'll see fruit, growth, depth, and change. Sometimes it will seem fast, sometimes it will seem slow. Sometimes you'll give more than you receive, and vice versa. It will be messy—and beautiful. And through it all, you'll each get to praise God as He makes you stronger together than any of you would be individually, through the spiritual "cross-pollination" of having many varieties of Christians, all growing together in devoted proximity to one another.

DAY 24

ANSWER
We live as a family when we depend on God, not ourselves.

READ
1 Corinthians 3:16–17

PRAY & PLAY

"IT IS FUN TO BE A CHRISTIAN."[7]

The words caught me off guard. Originally written by longtime minister and founder of World Harvest Mission Jack Miller to a struggling missionary in Uganda, I read them during a two-month sabbatical, which had been twice delayed by difficult seasons in our church. Miller's collection of letters from a seasoned minister to a variety of ministers was recommended as a source of refreshment and an example of perseverance after several months of feeling defeated by some of the hardest things I'd dealt with in sixteen years of ministry. There were many helpful words, examples, and exhortations in Miller's book—but this phrase was one I was utterly unprepared for.

I could have described the Christian life as being many things—but "fun" was not one of them. "Rich," "full of life," "blessed," or even "joyful"? Sure! But "fun"? That was new to me. It sent me on an occasional quest over the next few years, through which I started taking to heart that God instructs His people in both "a time to weep [and] . . . mourn," and also "a time to laugh [and]...dance" (Eccl. 3:4). Some creatures God created are just plain funny. And since Jesus was fully human, and thus experienced every human emotion, then He laughed like every other human on earth. On occasion His words involve sarcasm and irony, and the Bible is full of humorous stories, irony, and wordplay—even if much was lost in translation from the original languages.[8]

After so many invitations, topics, and charges to intentionality and devotion, and to taking this life of deep discipleship seriously, I want to close the book by guarding—and hopefully relieving—readers from taking everything *too* seriously: a good healthy family finds time to pray together, and a good healthy spiritual family takes time to play together.

CELEBRATE!

Some of my favorite times in ministry involve various teams pausing, looking back, and celebrating God's work over a past season or year. My church's elder couples get together once a month—sometimes with kids, sometimes without—and the time is largely spent having fun, remembering that we're sheep before we're shepherds, and taking a moment to celebrate God's goodness. These nights usually involve a good meal, good drinks, a lot of smiles, and often a game. In several passages of the gospel accounts, at the end of a long day of ministry and after the crowds have gone, we see Jesus sitting and talking with His smaller band of closest disciples. My mental image of this is a group of trusted friends sitting around a fire in the Judean countryside, weary but happy from the day's work. They're laughing, eating, discussing high and low points of the day, asking Jesus questions, and breathing deeply of God's goodness.

Whether this was the exact experience Jesus and His disciples had or not, it can be ours. We can rest in God; we can circle up after a long month of our respective counseling, preaching, conversations; and ministry, and we can enjoy God's goodness. That's some of what our elder team prioritized during those monthly gatherings.

For the first several years of our church we took all our leaders on a weekend retreat to accomplish a similar purpose: elder couples, ministry and organizational leaders, group leaders, and anyone who served in a regular role in our church would convene at a retreat center. We'd often do some training, but mostly we played sports and games, took walks and hikes, fished, prayed, ate, and drank together, and celebrated God's grace—in general ways across our church and in specific ways in each other. We had fun.

Every group I've ever been involved with also intentionally makes time for fun: from the annual Valentine's dinner or game nights mentioned earlier in the book, to movie nights, to holiday scavenger hunts in downtown Fort Worth, to watching playoff games or awards shows together, to meeting up at parks or local cultural events, dozens of moments exist throughout a given year in which we can—and must—just have fun. Especially for those of us who tend to take life more seriously, and who are used to every moment of "Christian activity" looking formal and planned, this will be both sanctifying and necessary—healthy families have fun; your spiritual family should too!

WE ARE GOD'S TEMPLE

One of the most striking scenes in the Bible is Jesus entering the Jerusalem temple, turning over tables, and rebuking those who profane the holiness of God's old covenant dwelling place: "Is it not written," Jesus charges, referring to Isaiah 56:7, "'My house shall be called a house of prayer for all the nations'? But you have made it a den of robbers" (Mark 11:17). If having fun reminds us that everything doesn't depend on us, intentionally becoming a household of prayer helps us remember that everything does depend on God.

In God's new covenant, there is no building in which His presence dwells. Welcoming Christians into the "house of God" to worship on a Sunday is actually a false teaching; in God's new covenant, His presence doesn't reside in a physical temple or any building. Rather, God's presence resides in the hearts of His people! We are each a "temple of the Holy Spirit" (1 Cor. 6:19). While each follower of Jesus is individually a "temple," where God's presence resides, a term God uses for His people collectively in the New Testament is "the household of God." Paul charges Christians in Galatia to "do good to everyone, and especially to those who are of the household of faith" (Gal. 6:10). He reminds Christians in Ephesus that they are "no longer strangers and aliens, but you are fellow citizens with the saints and members of the household of God" (Eph. 2:19). Most overtly, Paul expresses God's desire that Christians in Ephesus "may know how one ought to behave in the *household of God, which is the church of the living God*" (1 Tim. 3:15). We are God's temple, personally and collectively. His Spirit resides in every follower of Jesus. And whether gathered or scattered, we are God's household, stronger together.

Households of Prayer

While Jesus frees His people from needing to enter a certain building to find God or pray, God consistently calls His people to remain a people of prayer. Prayer—for each other, for needs, for God to save and grow people, for protection and provision, for guidance and deliverance, for a thousand other things, and above all for God's kingdom to come and His will to be done—declares our dependence on God to do what only God can do. Prayer displays our need for God; it admits our trust in His authority and power. Pursuing this level of depth with others cannot happen in a fruitful way without prayer. Pray for God to open eyes and soften hearts to this devoted life. Pray for God to bring the right people alongside you, to pursue it with you. Pray for vulnerability and openness, a Spirit-led commitment, and that He will help you all obey God together. Pray for each other, often—in celebrations and needs. Pray that He would produce fruit in each of you, in your communal life, and in your pursuit of His mission. And pray that His gospel, His kingdom, and His glory would be the priority, motivation, goal, and message of your spiritual family.

Different people pray for different things; we even learn to pray as we pray with others. God works through prayers. And God makes His people more aware of His will and His ways through prayers. So . . . as God's family, we must pray! Prayers don't have to be fancy, long, or eloquent. Like the rest of Christian life, they can be simple, normal aspects of our life together. Pray a ton before you form your group, pray a ton for your group, and pray a ton with your group. Trusting God and following Him into the life He invites us into begins with prayer. As we consider how to actually pursue this, we must start as a people—God's household—of prayer.

DECLARATIONS OF DEPENDENCE

In Matthew 28, Jesus reminds His followers that His great commission rests on His authority, not ours—"All authority in heaven and on earth has been given to me" (v. 18). It's up to Him, not us. And any making or maturing of disciples, baptizing and teaching, only occurs because of His power and presence in people's lives: "I am with [you all] always, to the end of the age" (v. 20). God's in charge; we're not. Jesus saves; we don't. Because of this, we can take the time to both pray and play with our spiritual families.

Playing and praying remind us that we rest in God's grace, that His burden is light, and that He created us with limits. When we play together, we deepen relationship and affection for each other and remember that the authority and power to accomplish anything good *doesn't* rest on our ability, seriousness, or control. When we pray together, we deepen our relationship and affection with God together, and remember that the authority and power to accomplish

101 WAYS
TO MOVE FROM FAÇADE TO FAMILY

93 Commute with spiritual siblings—whether a carpool or the same bus, use the time well.

94 If you have workspace flexibility, share space with others—split the rent, even, and save your organizations' money!

95 Spend your lunch hour with others—commit at least some days each week not to eat alone.

96 If your work has flexible hours, shape your schedule around others: share meals, help with kids, and simply spend time together.

anything good *does* rest on God's ability, seriousness, or control. So how do we make this life together actually happen? We pray and we play. We wrap up the book's content by reminding each other, "It's fun to be a Christian."

WEEK FIVE IN ACTION

The last day of each week you will read how churches across the world live as a family and will discuss this week's content with others. As you discuss the questions, be honest with yourself and others, and let them speak truth in love, as you put this book into practice together.

LIVING AS FAMILY: BIRESICA MISSIO DEI, BUCHAREST, ROMANIA

Three years ago, we decided to bring a child into our family (foster care leading to adoption) from a set of challenging circumstances. The child had significant health issues that would demand special attention and medical care. He was the sixth member of our family, and we needed a bigger car. We did not have any savings since we had spent all our money fixing our house we had just moved into. We were aware of all these realities, but also confident that God was bigger than our situation, and that our families and church family would be with us through this journey. Of course, God has used their support, prayers and practical help in ways we cannot describe. As our main practical need was a bigger car, we were overwhelmed one Sunday afternoon when we were handed [the equivalent of $10,000] by our families and church family. It was one way God used the church to remind us that He was taking care of us.

And by the way, we are not the only people in our church who have received money to buy a car. It is a habit of our church to spontaneously collect money for people who encounter various challenges and come alongside them in this and other ways. People are generous to give, sometimes with personal sacrifices and beyond their comfort zone.

We experience life as family in other small and simple ways too. Anyone with children knows that the arrival of a new family member brings not only joy and excitement but also new challenges, especially for the new mom. Sometimes our missional community cooks

101 WAYS TO MOVE FROM FAÇADE TO FAMILY

97 When someone has a financial burden, help meet it—as an interest-free loan with clear guidelines perhaps, or a gift.

98 If someone won't accept charity, pay them for odd jobs, even if you could do them yourself.

99 Use your business for others: if someone in your spiritual family is raising funds and you can influence your company's donations, support them.

100 Consider your job's impact on your spiritual family: how do the hours and commute impact others? Would you go as far as considering a change to give others more time?

101 Remember God's grace: This applies to every bit of this book, so it's a good one to end on. When—not if!—you mess up, miss a chance to "one another," offend someone, speak truth without love, or botch the gospel, simply remember grace, pursue forgiveness and reconciliation. Jesus was the only perfect human; the rest of us are being transformed into His likeness. And transformation is a long road.

meals for the family for a few weeks until the family figures out life in their new reality. The new mom gets help from other experienced moms—with feeding, caring for the child, dealing with health issues and fatigue, and so on. At critical moments like this, the help that families receive not only meets practical needs but also brings them closer to the family of God and to God Himself. They not only know that He loves and cares for them, but they experience this love and care through His people.

Adiel Bunescu

"HOW" QUESTIONS TO DISCUSS

- [ ] **GENERAL:** What impacted you most this week? What was new, convicting, difficult, or confusing? What biblical truths do you need others to remind you of, in love?
- [ ] **GENERAL:** Jesus summarizes the Old Testament Law into one command: "Love the Lord your God with all your heart and with all your soul and with all your mind and with all your strength [and] love your neighbor as yourself" (Mark 12:30–31). In this last week of the book, where do you need the most help in this deeply devoted life: heart (emotional capacity), soul (desire), mind (knowledge), or strength (capacity/ability), or love of neighbor? Why?
- [ ] **DAY 21:** Of the "thirds" of the gospel, which is/are easiest for you to believe and live out of, and which is/are hardest? How can others help your unbelief?
- [ ] **DAY 21:** How does the gospel free you from fear, doubt, selfishness, or insecurity to boldly, sacrificially follow God into new, deep devotion to a close spiritual family?
- [ ] **DAY 22:** Of the areas mentioned—finances, marriage/singleness, and parenting—which is hardest for you to let others into and why? What would it take to invite people in?

☐ **DAY 22:** What needs do you currently have: physical, emotional, spiritual, or otherwise? Who can help meet them, and how will you boldly bring them to him/her/them?

☐ **DAY 23:** What passions, gifts, experiences, learnings, etc. has God given you to build up others? Take some time to celebrate the unique grace and story He's given you.

☐ **DAY 23:** How could your close spiritual family shape several weeks of meetings around the various angles of discipleship and equipping discussed today? How will you plan for this?

☐ **DAY 24:** How much does your close spiritual family play together? What holds you back from doing so more, and how can your group grow in this area?

☐ **DAY 24:** How much does your close spiritual family prioritize praying together? What holds you back from doing so more, and how can your group grow in this area?

☐ **GENERAL:** As we end the book, what next steps will you commit to, personally and with others, to put some principles into practice and pursue the "devoted life" of a close spiritual family?

☐ **GENERAL:** Look over this week's "101 Ways." What else could you do, per your own gifting, spiritual family, and mission field, to live as God's family? Post ideas with the hashtag, #genuine community.

AFTERWORD: TO CHURCH LEADERS

Read: 1 Peter 5:1–5

Church leaders lead by fostering a familial culture.

"WHY WILL YOUR CHURCH GATHER ON A SUNDAY?"

It's a question I ask as we start each round of our church planting residency. Very few residents have thoughtful answers; most range from blank stares to some version of, "Well, it's what every church I know does!" "That," I often respond, "is a poor reason to gather!" My point isn't to go against Sunday gatherings or that historical tradition should be ignored. My point is that many leaders simply do what we've always known, rarely question the motive behind an action, and accept our experience as the norm. But many church leaders seem dissatisfied. Perhaps you yearn for your people to experience deeper relationships with God and each other. Perhaps you want more people to step up into ministry and leadership. Perhaps you pray for more fruit, more proactivity, more baptisms, and more discipleship. Many ministers long for better "results" (per se), but we feel trapped by the status quo. So we pursue change through a few tweaks, tips, and tricks to the existing vision, culture, and strategy. We get excited when momentum slightly increases, then—once the newness of the change, series, ministry, or vision statement wears off—we feel down as our people return to their lackluster, consumeristic ways.

What if it's not their fault? What if it's not yours either, but rather a natural result of the vision, culture, and systems most ministers have been shaped by? Back on Day 3, I explained the church growth movement, the philosophy that has increasingly shaped Western evangelicalism since the 1960s. I also introduced some dangers of that movement. I won't rehash that content here, but if we truly yearn for deeper commitment, discipleship, involvement, ownership, and spirituality in our people, and if those things aren't being produced in the water we're currently asking them to swim in, is it time to change the water?

As a fellow elder, with a deep love for local churches and a deep concern for the future of global Christianity, I humbly offer three shifts as you (re-?) instill a depth of Christian life together. Please pause before you go on and read 1 Peter 5:1–5, which is our starting point for leading God's people (not yours!) away from settling for a religious façade to living as a devoted spiritual family.

GIVE AWAY RESPONSIBILITY . . . AND AUTHORITY

The first shift involves giving away responsibility and, at times, authority. If we're honest, some forms of the "shameful gain" Peter describes that commonly drive church leaders are our influence over others, the platforms that build our mini-kingdoms, or the accolades we get as people receive the words we give them on Sundays. Even while saying things like, "We want people to prioritize everyday discipleship" and "Group life is important," if the majority of a church's budget, staff time, and energy go into Sunday gatherings, our people see through our words and know what truly matters to us. Or, if we say we want to develop leaders but limit them to specific ministry lanes we create and continually spoon-feed them content, format, and directives "from the top," are we really helping them thrive as leaders? Or are we just equipping them to be servants to *our* kingdoms, keeping all responsibility and authority to ourselves? Part of every church's calling is to "equip the saints for the work of ministry" (Eph. 4:12). As "nonprofessional" people actually start participating in this work though, it means others might come to us less—and frankly, that can be hard for us!

Giving away responsibility also means giving away control: "But what if they blow it?" No one is ever ready to counsel, preach, start a ministry, or serve until they can actually get their hands dirty doing it! In Jesus' parable of the talents, a landowner gave away actual funds to his servants—that's risky. One servant did poorly with the money, but the others proved themselves ready for more responsibility. The master maintained authority in most of the story, but he knew the long-term gain was worth giving away actual responsibility. In the end, he was confidently able to give actual authority to those servants who did well (see Matt. 25:14–30).

Equipping the saints means helping God's people discover, and thrive in, their gifts. It means apprenticing them and giving them knowledge *and* hands-on responsibility to help them grow. It means stepping back so they can step forward. It might even mean people leaving your group, or even your church (is it yours?), as we affirm other leaders in our church, or send them to plant/lead another church. Will we risk some responsibility (and for some, a misplaced identity in being the person everyone needs), to equip others to take true ministry responsibility? Can we then give away real authority, sharing our decisions, pulpits, ministerial duties, and even God's people (not ours) with others, for the long-term benefit of His kingdom (not ours)?

PURSUE DEPTH OVER WIDTH

A second shift is from going wider with more people to going deeper with fewer. Many church leaders find that one of the hardest aspects of our role is being content with the people God has given us: "If they were just more (or less) . . . [something]," some secretly lament, filling in the blank with any number of desires; some holy and others far from it. The church growth movement pushes ministers to value "more": more people, more giving, more services, more-more-more. While a desire for new disciples in our churches is a good thing, Peter's charge names church leaders' top priority: "shepherd the flock of God *that is among you*" (1 Peter 5:2). In other words, "Love *these people*, not those you wish you had," God might say, "reflect my heart in meeting each individual and situation, exactly where they are in their journey. As a good under-shepherd, follow the Chief Shepherd's example: nourish and care for them, protect them, lead them to good water. Over time, teach them to feed themselves, and to shepherd others. But 'feed my sheep'—be content with the exact ones I have given you to steward on my behalf" (see John 21:15–17).

By God's grace, He delegated to church leaders some of His flock. Are we shepherding them well and building His kingdom, or are we squandering the responsibility He's given us, or abdicating the "oversight" shepherds are charged with, or ministering "under compulsion," or longing for different pastures or easier sheep?

If so, we are more the servants in Jesus' parable of the talents rather than the master. Would Jesus—the Chief Shepherd—observe the ways we steward His people and how we carry out the responsibilities He's given us, and deem us ready for more? Like the landowner in His parable, Jesus maintains "all authority"; in fact, our role is to "plant" and "water" like Paul and Apollos, but "only God gives the growth." Jesus alone "will build his church," so rather than aim for shallow and more, what if we pursued going deeper with fewer (even if "our" churches stay smaller, and we never get noticed or famous)?[1]

TOPPLE THE PEDESTAL

A third shift in helping grow your church's life together is to "clothe yourselves . . . with humility" and increasingly be "among" your people as "examples to the flock." One of the most unique things I see in many churches is a declared vision for the body's involvement, but a continued priority of "the professionals" as the only people who can, for example, handle God's Word, distribute communion elements, teach, and lead ministries. How can people be involved like we say we want if our actions keep them removed from involvement? Start with small shifts: move small group discussions from Sunday sermons to biblical texts (in other words, from a preacher's imperfect words to God's perfect Word) and find ways to help people in your church pray, sing, or engage the Bible outside of church-sponsored gatherings, groups, or classes.

A theme of the Protestant Reformation was that "the church" (and specifically its priests) had replaced Christ as the means of distributing God's grace. Have we honestly moved away from that? Or do we keep God's people reliant on professional preachers to give them God's Word, and professional musicians to create the only method of worship? After all, one of the endeavors of Martin Luther, a Reformation leader, was to put the Bible in the hands of everyday Christians—and in their own language—so they could know God and read and obey His Word directly.

Many church leaders find themselves on the top of a proverbial pedestal. Whether we put ourselves there or people put us there, "clergy" are viewed as a step above "laity," in relationship with God and holiness. The larger a church gets, the further removed leaders can get from "the flock of God." The pedestal climbs higher and higher. "God opposes the proud but gives grace to the humble" (1 Peter 5:5). The bad fruit of this clergy-laity divide is increasingly displayed as God seems to push more and more pedestals out from under prideful, "famous," and once-sought-after church leaders. A common theme in announcements of church leaders' disqualification goes something like this: "He removed himself from community" or "He stopped listening to others [or] accepting accountability." Church leaders, let's topple the pedestal ourselves, while it's still low: let's be the lead confessors and repenters. Let's share honestly about our sin, weakness, and need for others. Let's celebrate aspects of faith that others—everyday followers of Jesus in our close spiritual families—are more mature than us, and how they benefit us personally as we all grow up in Christ together! We're sheep before we're shepherds, after all; we're imperfect and weak, in need of God's perfection and strength. Let's live humbly, as imperfect "examples to the flock" pursuing all the same values, devotion, repentance, and lives we call our fellow sheep to.

CHANGE THE CULTURE

These three shifts are about changing your church's culture. Leadership posture, time spent calling people to churchy events, and the ways we direct church funds are all part of our culture. The words we use, job descriptions we write, and goals we set are too. So are the ways we preach and the applications we give, the way people connect to our church and to ministries, the level of commitment we ask, and literally every other thing we do. No matter the vision we cast, if the culture we create screams something different, people always believe their experience over the words we say.

So for example, we cannot say we want people to spend time with each other and on mission, then fill the calendar with churchy events. We cannot say we want more peer discipleship if we don't equip people to take responsibility for each other. We cannot say we want people to know their Bible more if the only way they receive it is from a preacher's mouth. And so on. Missiologist Dr. JR Woodward defines the elements of culture as the *language* we use, the *artifacts* we use and create, the *narrative* we live by that shapes us, the *rituals* we practice, the *institutions* that give us stability (like structures and systems), and the *ethics* that stem from our beliefs and form how we live.[2] Each of these elements, and the metrics we measure and celebrate, shapes our churches and molds our people in some way. If we say we yearn for deeper commitment, discipleship, involvement, ownership, and spirituality in our people that isn't being produced in the water we're currently asking them to swim in, are we willing to throw out the dirty water, replace it with fresh, and make the necessary cultural changes?

A DIAGNOSTIC AND FURTHER RESOURCES

If you need help diagnosing your church's culture in the early 2020s—to see if your ministry is more institutionalized, professionalized, and centralized (vs. familial, personal, and equipping-focused, and involving everyone in ministry)—consider your church's response to COVID: when unable to gather physically, many churches primarily attempted to recreate a distribution method to deliver sermons and content to people. By contrast, other churches redistributed their staff duties to check in on people, form new groups online, and equip leaders as the front lines of discipleship and mission, giving people responsibility for serving each other. This contrast—a one-direction message distribution vs. a multifaceted equipping of saints—displays what the churches prioritize as vital ministry and discipleship. If you're reading this well past the COVID season, simply consider where your church's budget and staff time go (programs/events vs. people/equipping), strategic goals and metrics (Do you celebrate "input metrics" more, or "output"?), and fruit (Who's doing the ministry? Are disciples being made?).

Obviously shepherding your flock to become a spiritual family takes prayer, time, and intentionality. One "afterword" and one book cannot accomplish this feat! But as God produces good fruit, our team at Moody developed resources to serve you on that journey. First, this book is written for group settings over five weeks. Second, at genuinecommunity.net you'll find "next steps plan" for groups, six weeks of sermon outlines, and graphics, teaching videos, and other suggestions. These can help church leaders and those involved in your church's group take tangible steps toward the devoted lives God invites His people into.

I started a church in 2009, and we have pursued this kind of life ever since. It's hard and messy—and really beautiful. As people become honest with each other, sin is revealed and must be dealt with. Giving away responsibility can backfire. People with authority can abuse it. As it turns out, "the heart is deceitful above all things, and desperately sick; who can understand it?" (Jer. 17:9). But many followers of Jesus yearn to play a part in God's mission, and, by His Spirit, are able and gifted to step into whatever role among the flock God created them for. New believers and young people thrive when they realize they matter and can use their gifts for the good of "more mature" people (in both faith and age). God has a role for all His people to play, in His Church, mission, and kingdom. I hope you'll prayerfully and excitedly join me to equip the flock God has given you to live as deeply devoted, vital and valued, known and loved, members of a close spiritual family. After all, that is the life God invites us into and empowers us for, for our mutual good and His glory, as we remove façades and pursue a biblical, Spirit-filled life as members of the spiritual family of God.

APPENDIX A: SHARING YOUR STORY[1]

A helpful "first step" to take in getting to know others more deeply is intentionally learning each other's stories. This is true whether you have walked with people for a long while or whether you just formed a new group. Knowing each other sets you up well, adds a level of comfort, and gives each other a sense of permission to speak honestly with each other as your group starts pursuing relational depth together. A strong foundation for known-ness is hearing each other share their stories, listening for their hearts and God's work, and responding with good questions, care, celebration, and prayer.

But sharing our stories can be hard. We might not know what to share or what is most important. We have a hard time condensing many years into five minutes. And sometimes we don't want to share some parts of our story. In the *Gospel Fluency Handbook*, my co-author Jeff Vanderstelt and I suggest two methods to help group members share our stories together.

- ➜ Method 1—"Instagram Stories": Draw five or six boxes, which will represent different parts of your story. Draw a still frame picture that captures the essence of that part, then prepare to walk your group through the boxes. It doesn't matter how good your drawings are; this is simply a way for you to tell your story, to share it with others.[2]
- ➜ Method 2—"Pillars": Reflect on three to four key events in your life, which significantly shaped, influenced, and directed other elements of your life. Write about the events, situations, or people surrounding each, and prepare to explain to your group why and how each has shaped your life.[3]

→ Group response: With either method, the only stipulation is that you be honest—even let yourself be stretched in vulnerability! As your group listens to each other's stories, listen for and then celebrate ways that God has worked. Listen for themes of where identity is found, of what problems keep arising, of where hope lies, and what functional redeemers exist. Ask questions and point out these themes in love. And above all, celebrate areas of life where God and His truth are known, trusted, and believed.

For more resources on sharing your story and the gospel, visit saturatetheworld.com/gf and saturatetheworld.com/dna-resources.

APPENDIX B: ASKING GOOD QUESTIONS[1]

Asking good questions helps us know and understand themes, questions, fears, idols, and struggles in each other's lives, as well as celebrations and joys.

HOW DO I ASK GOOD QUESTIONS AS A GOSPEL SHEPHERD?

- ➜ We must be led by the Holy Spirit! It's His job to bring conviction, and He is the primary shepherd. He alone knows the depths of a person's heart, and He will guide us as we lovingly pursue people with good questions. Pray before, during, and after any shepherding conversation, asking the Spirit to speak.
- ➜ Often the Spirit will provide great questions immediately after a conversation. Write these down for future reference.
- ➜ Ask lots of questions throughout the conversation, especially in the beginning. We like to say, "Ask ten questions for every pronouncement."
- ➜ Ask open-ended questions that can't be answered with "yes" or "no," as these questions do not provide much information and can leave room for us to make assumptions about the answer.
- ➜ Sometimes the best question is not a question. "Tell me more . . ." is a great way to invite a person to tell more about what's going on in their heart.

SOME GOOD QUESTIONS TO USE

The following is adapted from Paul Tripp's *Instruments in the Redeemer's Hands*.[2]

- What? Ask people to define their terms. "What did you mean when you said . . . ?"
- How? Ask people to clarify what they mean with concrete, real life examples. "How did that situation unfold? Give us some more detail."
- Where? and When? Ask people to provide more information about the details and the order of events. "Where were you when this happened? When did this happen?"
- How often? Ask people to describe the frequency of their struggles. Ask them about themes and patterns. "How often do you do this?"
- Why? Ask people to explain why they responded as they did in a given situation. Ask the person to share their reasons, values, purposes, and desires. "Why were you feeling frustrated?"

A WORD ABOUT "WHY?"

"Why?" is a great question because it helps uncover the motives of the heart. We sometimes refer to "Why?" as the Why Shovel, because it helps us dig around to get to the root of a problem. However, a few cautions should be noted.

- "Why?" can sound condescending, judgmental, and even rhetorical (a question that's asked where the answer is so obvious that the question itself helps prove a point). "Why on earth did you do that?" clearly implies that the person asking the question thinks a poor decision was made. The question does not invite an honest, vulnerable response.
- Also, "Why?" is sometimes used as a one-word question, which can sound accusatory and does not invite an open dialogue. If a wife says to her husband, "I'm feeling sad and

frustrated," and he responds by simply asking, "Why?" she is likely to perceive that he is upset because she is feeling sad and wants to hear her reason so he can refute it.

→ "Why?" can be a powerful tool that must be wielded with wisdom and sensitivity of the Spirit.

For a fantastic list of more specific questions, I also recommend Dr. David Powlison's "X-Ray Questions."[3] I use them often in group settings, as well as counseling, parenting, and even everyday conversations.

For more resources on asking good questions, visit saturatetheworld.com/dna-resources.

APPENDIX C: APPLYING GOSPEL ANSWERS

These two exercises introduce ways to speak the good news of Jesus into everyday lives, stories, and situations. As you practice applying gospel answers to hypothetical situations, it becomes easier to apply similar answers to your group members' real-life situations.

EXERCISE #1: JESUS IS THE BETTER ____[1]

Pick some characters/roles from the list below. In the middle column, write a few words about how he/she did/didn't/does/doesn't fulfill his/her role. In the right column describe how Jesus perfectly fulfilled the person's role, in a way they never could, to the glory of God.

EXERCISE #2: GOD'S STORY[2]

If we don't view life through the lens of God's story, we view it in light of a lesser story.

The first column below lists dominant questions asked by each movement of God's story. The second column lists objective, biblical answers to those questions that come when God's story is our dominant story. In the third column, write a few areas of disbelief you struggle with. In the final column, consider alternative narratives that reinforce this area of unbelief. What story are you believing instead of the story of God?

EXERCISE #1: JESUS IS THE BETTER ___

JESUS IS THE BETTER . . .	HUMAN IN THAT ROLE	JESUS IN THAT ROLE
Adam	Adam failed the test in the garden and gave into temptation.	Jesus passed the test by overcoming the tempter and submitting himself in the garden of Gethsemane.
Abel		
Abraham		
Isaac		
Jacob		
Joseph		
Moses		
Job		
David		
Esther		
Jonah		
For further development in this skill, compare Jesus to inanimate objects too: the rock of Moses, manna, the temple, light, water, and more.		

EXERCISE #2: GOD'S STORY

	QUESTION	OBJECTIVE/BIBLICAL ANSWER
CREATION	Where is my identity? What do I look to, trust in, depend on, for my worth?	Child of God, created in His image; my identity is in Christ alone; I am reliant/dependent on Him
FALL	What is wrong? What is the real problem/issue?	Sin Rejection of God Brokenness that's part of living in a fallen world
REDEMPTION	What can fix this?	Jesus
NEW CREATION	Where is hope? In what is my confidence found?	God's promises shown through history Eternity/Jesus' return

AREA OF DISBELIEF	POSSIBLE "FALSE" ANSWERS/STORY

After you've tried this for yourself, pick a few other hypothetical scenarios and write potential answers for each: perhaps a new spouse, a parent of a rebellious teen, an environmental activist, someone who can't stop dwelling on their rough past, an older single woman/man, or someone you actually know, in a real struggle/issue they're having.

For more resources on speaking the truth in love
and printable versions of these pages,
visit saturatetheworld.com/gf.

ACKNOWLEDGMENTS

Books are a collaborative effort. Given this one's topic, I'm especially glad to celebrate those whose gifts, perspectives, edits, and stories came together to shape it.

To Jess, Char, Mags, and Trav, thank you for your sacrifice and willingness, not only for time to write but for pursuing this inconvenient and selfless—but fun and fruitful—way of life together. To the Loyd and Connelly clans, it's a joy to pursue life in Christ with literal family who is also our spiritual family and close friends. To the individuals and couples who have walked closely with me and my family throughout the years, God has used you to shape this book but also to grow us more than you'll ever know.

I'm honored to share examples throughout this book of how life in a spiritual family can look. To those whose names appear in these pages, thank you for giving yourself to the depth of relationship God shaped us for. Thank you, Shaun, for the foreword; Abe and Jeff for the appendices; and leaders from six cultures for helping us glimpse the unified principles and diverse practices, of pursuing this life in various churches and contexts. For ten years, members of The City Church—and now those planting Salt+Light Community—have taught and lived this content. So have church members I knew growing up and sisters and brothers across the Soma Family and on our Saturate team. Some of this book's words likely came from some of you but have become so ingrained that I neglected to give you credit. Please accept my sincere apology and deep gratitude!

Tina, Ben, and Darryl spoke into the manuscript, alongside others who shaped specific parts of it. And a great professional team rounds out this list of collaborators: Thank you, Don, for representation. And thank you, Moody team members—Amy, Mackenzie, Connor, and others—for lending specific gifts, skills, and passion, to create and craft this book. Echoing Christian life in general, this book is better because of each of you than it would be alone.

Above all, I'm grateful to God our Father for making us children; to Christ our Brother for modeling perfect life, sacrificing so wayward siblings have a way home, rising to give new and eternal hope, and promising to return and fully restore our familial relationships; and to God the Spirit who teaches, convicts, empowers, and otherwise helps us live this countercultural life now, a foretaste of eternal life together. Every glimpse of a perfect, diverse, unified family starts and ends with, and happens through, the triune family that is our God. "To him be glory in the church and in Christ Jesus throughout all generations, forever and ever. Amen" (Eph. 3:21).

NOTES

START HERE: "Y'ALL"

1. "US Becoming Less Religious: Modest Drop in Overall Rates of Belief and Practice, but Religiously Affiliated Americans Are as Observant as Before," Pew Research Center, November 3, 2015, https://www.pewforum.org/2015/11/03/u-s-public-becoming-less-religious/.
2. Dietrich Bonhoeffer, *Life Together* (London: SCM Press, 2015), 11–12, italics added.
3. "2842. Koinónia," Bible Hub, https://biblehub.com/greek/2842.htm.
4. Darryl Eyb, email to author, August 12, 2020.
5. See Rom. 12; 1 Cor. 12; Eph. 2; 1 Peter 2; 1 Cor. 3.
6. See Eph. 5 and Rev. 19.
7. See 2 Cor. 6 and 1 Tim. 5.
8. See Matt. 12 and 1 Tim. 5.
9. See Gal. 6 and Eph. 2.

WEEK ONE: WHY SHOULD I EVEN CARE?

1. Facebook Groups. (2020). *Found by the Hounds* [Television commercial]. Retrieved from https://youtu.be/cTRR92URXpo.
2. The training I attended is called "Soma School," and now occurs in churches across the world. If you want to experience this kind of church family in action today, see wearesoma.com/soma-school/.
3. Aaron Sorkin et al., *The West Wing*, 1x19, "Let Bartlet Be Bartlet," aired April 26, 2000, on NBC.
4. Soong-Chan Rah, *The Next Evangelicalism: Freeing the Church from Western Cultural Captivity* (Downers Grove, IL: InterVarsity, 2009), 95.
5. Ibid., 96.
6. Ibid., 92.
7. Bill Hendricks, "The Origin of Executive Pastors," XPastor, April 7, 2018, https://www.xpastor.org/new-xp/essentials/the-origin-of-executive-pastors/.
8. Eph. 4:12.
9. Elliot Grudem, personal conversation, Leaders Collective Church Planters Gathering, April 2019.
10. David Foster Wallace, "This Is Water," speech given at Kenyon College, May 21, 2005. Learn more: http://bulletin-archive.kenyon.edu/x4280.html.
11. Russ Rainey, "Willow Creek Reveal Study - A Summary," The Christian Coaching Center, http://www.christiancoachingcenter.org/index.php/russ-rainey/coachingchurch2/.

12. John Mark Comer, *The Ruthless Elimination of Hurry: How to Stay Emotionally Healthy and Spiritually Alive in the Chaos of the Modern World* (Colorado Springs: WaterBrook: 2019), 265.

13. Jack Haywood, ed., *NKJV, Spirit-Filled Life Bible*, 3rd ed. (Nashville: Thomas Nelson, 2018).

14. See Ps. 103:13; 1 John 3:1; James 1:17; Prov. 3:11; Matt. 6:26; John. 12:26; Matt. 6:6.

15. The most common examples of addressing God individually are when Jesus addresses His Father in prayer.

16. WeAreSoma, "Soma School Notes" (Tacoma, WA: unpublished, 2014), 11. https://wearesoma.com/wp-content/uploads/2018/06/Soma-School-Final.pdf.

17. "Our DNA," Blueprint Church, https://www.blueprintchurch.org/our-dna, accessed May 6, 2020.

18. WeAreSoma, "Soma School Notes," 11.

19. Rabbi Jonathan Gross, "How Much Would the Mishkan Cost Today?," Orthodox Union, February 16, 2016, https://www.ou.org/life/torah/how-much-would-the-mishkan-cost-today/. Other authors calculate the total cost at over double that.

WEEK TWO: WHO IS MY SPIRITUAL FAMILY?

1. Suzanne Degges-White, "How Many Friends Do You Really Need in Adulthood?," *Psychology Today*, August 9, 2019, https://www.psychologytoday.com/us/blog/lifetime-connections/201908/how-many-friends-do-you-really-need-in-adulthood.

2. Ibid.

3. Maria Konnikova, "The Limits of Friendship," *New Yorker*, October 7, 2014 https://www.newyorker.com/science/maria-konnikova/social-media-affect-math-dunbar-number-friendships.

4. See studies like Aaron Earls, "The Church Growth Gap: The Big Get Bigger While the Small Get Smaller," *Christianity Today*, March 6, 2019: https://www.christianitytoday.com/news/2019/march/lifeway-research-church-growth-attendance-size.html.

5. Ed Stetzer, "Do You Know What Keeps Your Church from Growing?," EdStetzer.com, https://edstetzer.com/breaking-200.

6. Jeffrey Kranz, "All the 'One Another' Commands in the NT [Infographic]," Overview Bible, March 9, 2014, https://overviewbible.com/one-another-infographic/. Carl F. George, *Prepare Your Church for the Future* (Tarrytown: Revell, 1991), 129–31.

7. Mark 12:28–34, 9:50; Rom. 15:14; Gal. 6:2; Eph. 5:21; James 5:16; Eph. 4:15.

8. Rom. 12:10; 1 Cor. 12:25; Gal. 5:13; Gal. 6:2; Eph. 4:32; Rom. 12:16; 1 Peter 4:9; 1 John 3:11 (all NIV).

9. Michael Finkel, "Into the Woods: How One Man Survived Lone in the Wilderness for 27 Years," *Guardian*, March 15, 2017, https://www.theguardian.com/news/2017/mar/15/stranger-in-the-woods-christopher-knight-hermit-maine.

10. Ibid.

11. Michael Finkel, *The Stranger in the Woods: The Extraordinary Story of the Last True Hermit* (New York: Knopf, 2017), 90.

12. Ibid., 143.

13. Ron Hall and Denver Moore, *Same Kind of Different As Me* (Colorado Springs: Thomas Nelson, 2006), 132.

14. Martin Luther King Jr., Interview on *Meet the Press*, aired April 17, 1960, on CBS.

15. See Ps. 127:3; Mark 10:13–15; James 1:27, among many other examples.

16. Dave Wright, "A Brief History of Youth Ministry," The Gospel Coalition, April 2, 2012, https://www.thegospelcoalition.org/article/a-brief-history-of-youth-ministry/.

17. Ibid.

18. Aaron Earls, "Most Teenagers Drop Out of Church as Young Adults," LifeWay Research, January 15, 2019. https://lifewayresearch.com/2019/01/15/most-teenagers-drop-out-of-church-as-young-adults/.

19. Dave Wright, "A Brief History."

20. See, e.g., Neh. 12:43; Matt. 14:21; 15:38.

21. See, e.g., Acts 16:31–34; 18:8.

WEEK THREE: WHAT DOES A SPIRITUAL FAMILY DO?

1. Ray Ortlund, "Tenderhearted," The Gospel Coalition, October 5, 2011, https://www.thegospelcoalition.org/blogs/ray-ortlund/tenderhearted/.

2. Jeffrey Kranz, "All the 'One Another' Commands in the NT [Infographic]" Overview Bible, March 9, 2014, https://overviewbible.com/one-another-infographic/.

3. All the names in this sentence have been changed.

4. Cameron Crowe, *Jerry Maguire* (Culver City, CA: Columbia TriStar Home Video, 1999).

5. Wendy Harris: "Friends Help Each Other," *Daniel Tiger's Neighborhood*, ep. 107. The Fred Rogers Company: first aired on PBS September 10, 2012.

6. Think, for example, of everything from James Taylor's classic "You've Got a Friend" to Bruno Mars's catchy "Count on Me" to Kasey Musgraves's cheeky "Family Is Family"; from Josh Groban's crooning "You'll Never Walk Alone" to Israel Houghton's soulful "Others" to *High School Musical*'s "We're All in This Together."

7. See for example, Rosaria Butterfield's *The Gospel Comes with a House Key: Practicing Radically Ordinary Hospitality in Our Post-Christian World* (Wheaton, IL: Crossway, 2018).

8. Arthur C. Brooks, *Love Your Enemies: How Decent People Can Save America from the Culture of Contempt* (New York: Broadside Books, 2019), 33–34, italics added.

9. Ps. 23:1; 1 Peter 5:4, 1:19; John 21:17; Acts 20:28; Matt. 25:33.

10. "4166. poimén," Bible Hub, https://biblehub.com/greek/4166.htm.

11. "4165. poimainó" Bible Hub, https://biblehub.com/str/greek/4165.htm. Italics and bracketed phrase mine.

12. See 1 Peter 5:4. Most overtly, Paul charges elders in Ephesus, "Pay careful attention to yourselves and to all the flock, in which the Holy Spirit has made you *overseers* [ἐπισκόπους, title], to *care for* [ποιμαίνειν, verb; literally 'to shepherd'] the church of God" (Acts 20:28, italics mine). Peter writes to "the *elders* [πρεσβυτέρους, title] among you, as a *fellow elder* [συμπρεσβύτερος, title] and a witness of the sufferings of Christ, as well as a partaker in the glory that is going to be revealed: *shepherd* [ποιμάνατε, verb] the flock of God that is among you" (1 Peter 5:1–2).

13. Harold Sinkbeil, "Pastor as Sheepdog: Working Hard but Wagging His Tail": Logos, June 14, 2019, https://blog.logos.com/2019/06/pastor-as-sheepdog-working-hard-but-wagging-his-tail/.

14. Phil. 4:7; Heb. 3:13; Titus 1:9.

15. Matt. 7:15.

16. Prov. 27:6.

WEEK FOUR: WHEN AND WHERE DOES A SPIRITUAL FAMILY INTERACT?

1. "Values, Vision, and Mission," Doxa Church, https://www.doxa-church.com/valuesvisionmission.
2. See for example most of Jesus' public teaching, as well as the apostles' open-air proclamations of Jesus as Lord throughout Acts.
3. See as one example, Ather Fawaz, "'The Most Precious Resource We All Have Is Time,' Tweets Tim Cook in Memory of Steve Jobs," Neowin, October 5, 2019, https://www.neowin.net/news/the-most-precious-resource-we-all-have-is-time-tweets-tim-cook-in-memory-of-steve-jobs/.
4. Francis Chan, *Letters to the Church* (Colorado Springs: David C Cook, 2018), 53.
5. Peter Ocko et al., *The Office*, 7x7, "Christening", aired November 4, 2010, on NBC.
6. Francis Schaeffer, "The Mark of the Christian," *Christianity Today*, September 11, 1970, 7.
7. Marvin Olasky, "A Wave Came In," *World* Magazine, April 23, 2010, https://world.wng.org/2010/04/a_wave_came_in.
8. Shakespeare, Billy: *Romeo & Juliet*: Act II, Scene II.
9. C. H. Spurgeon, The Metropolitan Tabernacle Pulpit Sermons, vol. 54 (London: Passmore & Alabaster, 1908), 476–77.

WEEK FIVE: HOW DO WE START?

1. I first heard this term from Dr. Michael Goheen in a private lecture: "Probing a Missional Hermeneutic: Mission as a Central Interest and Goal of Biblical Story" (Vancouver, B.C., Canada), https://slideplayer.com/slide/7293006/.
2. John Calvin, *Institutes of the Christian Religion* (Grand Rapids, MI: Eerdmans, 2009). I.11.8
3. Jeff Christopherson, "The Road Ahead: 10 Characteristics of a Future Church Planter, Part 1," The Exchange (blog), *Christianity Today*, October 28, 2019, https://www.christianitytoday.com/edstetzer/2019/october/road-ahead-10-characteristics-future-church-planter-1.html.
4. See Rom. 12; 1 Cor. 12; Eph. 4.
5. See 1 Tim. 2.
6. Much of Jesus' ministry displays this, as do passages like Deut. 6, Acts 2, and Acts 4.
7. C. John Miller, *The Heart of a Servant Leader: Letters from Jack Miller* (Phillipsburg, NJ: P&R Publishing, 2004), 51.
8. See for more on this, Donald Sweeting, "The Humor of Christ." National Association of Evangelicals, Fall 2013, https://www.nae.net/the-humor-of-christ/.

AFTERWORD: TO CHURCH LEADERS

1. See 1 Peter 5:4; 1 Cor. 3:5–8; Matt. 16:18.

2. Summarized from JR Woodward, *Creating a Missional Culture*, (Downers Grove, IL: IVP, 2012), 35–39.

APPENDIX A: SHARING YOUR STORY

1. Here are two resources to help you go deeper in sharing your story: "God's Story: Our Dominant Story," Saturate, 2017, https://saturatetheworld.com/wp-content/uploads/2017/08/saturate-gfhandbook-dominant_story.pdf and "How to Share Your Story," Saturate, 2016, https://saturatetheworld.com/wp-content/uploads/2016/06/How-to-Share-Your-Story-V1.pdf.
2. The printable template is available at saturatetheworld.com/gf/week-6-instagram/.
3. A printable template is available at https://saturatetheworld.com/gf/week-6-three-pillars/.

APPENDIX B: ASKING GOOD QUESTIONS

1. "Gospel Shepherding: Asking Good Questions," Saturate, 2017, https://saturatetheworld.com/wp-content/uploads/2017/05/Gospel-Shepherding-Ask-Good-Questions.pdf.
2. Paul Tripp, *Instruments in the Redeemer's Hands* (Phillipsburg, NJ: P&R Publishing, 2002), 170–78.
3. David Powlison, *Seeing with New Eyes: Counseling and the Human Condition through the Lens of Scripture* (Phillipsburg, NJ: P&R Publishing, 2003), 129–44.

APPENDIX C: APPLYING GOSPEL ANSWERS

1. "Jesus is the Better ____," Saturate, 2017, https://saturatetheworld.com/wp-content/uploads/2017/08/saturate-gfhandbook-jesus-is-the-better.pdf
2. "God's Story: Our Dominant Story," Saturate.

FREE RESOURCES TO GO DEEPER

GENUINECOMMUNITY.NET

Ben Connelly and the team at Saturate (saturatetheworld.com) have created free resources to help leaders equip your church, organization, or group to dive deeper into genuine, gospel-formed community. We encourage you to explore them as you read, reflect, and process through this book, personally or with your group.

At genuinecommunity.net, you'll find:

- **Six weeks of customizable sermon outlines and slide decks**
- **Discussion Guides for leaders**
- **Printouts and exercises for you and your group**
- **Graphics and promotional materials**
- **Info on bulk orders**
- **Info on live or online training for your church or team**
- **And access to more free and paid resources**

LEARN MORE: GENUINECOMMUNITY.NET

GO SOCIAL:

As you post ideas, thoughts, pictures, and practices online, use the hashtag #genuinecommunity